THE
DEADLIEST
TRAIN WRECKS
OF
NEW ENGLAND

THE
DEADLIEST
TRAIN WRECKS
OF
NEW ENGLAND

GREGG M. TURNER

THE
History
PRESS

Published by The History Press
Charleston, SC
www.historypress.com

First published 2024

Manufactured in the United States

ISBN 9781467155540

Library of Congress Control Number: 2023948351

Notice: The information in this book is true and complete to the best of our knowledge. It is offered without guarantee on the part of the author or The History Press. The author and The History Press disclaim all liability in connection with the use of this book.

For my amazing sister, Melinda Ainsworth, and her late husband, Richard.

The drama that is virtually inherent in the operation of trains on steel rails has for its climatic third act the horrifying scenes of disasters, chiefly those of collisions and derailments. No tragedies of American life have so fastened themselves on our imagination.

—*Stewart H. Holbrook,* The Story of American Railroads

By the Author

CONTENTS

CONTENTS

PREFACE

While I was writing about railway history for nearly forty years, it was inevitable to encounter that unpleasant, perhaps most dreaded subject of all: train wrecks, accidents and disasters. Despite the subject's unsettling nature, the idea of authoring a book about them that occurred in New England had periodically interested me, for two reasons: because so little on the subject has ever been published and because their stories have largely vanished from the public's consciousness. Hopefully, this work will help correct those deficiencies.

Shortly after beginning the serious research, I discovered that literally hundreds upon hundreds of such events had taken place in New England since railroading began here in the 1830s. A great many were minor in nature with little or no loss of life and minimal damage to company property. Other events, however, extracted a greater toll, while still others had horrific consequences. Realizing that no single book could possibly recount them all in narrative form, I decided to focus on one category: *the deadliest of those wrecks, specifically those that claimed at least a dozen lives or more*. Eighteen such events are capsulized in the pages ahead.

That train wrecks still make for news cannot be argued. As author Lionel Holt states in *Red for Danger*, "Governments may fall or battles fought and lost, but no matter what the crisis of the hour may be a train derailment or collision involving even a small loss of life will be sure to command a banner headline in the popular Press." In truth, such events have punctuated world railway history ever since the industry emerged in distant England. In fact, at the ceremonial opening in September 1830 of the first intercity company, the Liverpool and Manchester Railway, the famous steam locomotive *Rocket*, while pulling an inaugural train, struck a Member of Parliament who was attempting to enter the carriage of a stopped train. The distinguished personage—Huskisson by name—died later that day and became the first casualty of the Railway Age. An insufficient locomotive brake had caused the accident.

Insufficient brakes on locomotives and cars would cause untold numbers of railway wrecks in England, America and elsewhere, and not until a continuous air braking system for trains evolved did this accident rate dramatically fall. But improper brakes were hardly the only reason railway disasters took place. Among the plethora of other causes were derailments, defective rails, broken car axles, poor construction and maintenance issues, faulty bridge designs, train dispatcher and telegraph operator errors, misinterpretation of train orders and signals by train crews, misplaced switches, objects left on tracks, boiler explosions, speeding, weather, washouts, sleep-deprived and intoxicated workers, trespassers, livestock, stalled vehicles on tracks and Acts of God. Fortunately, many of these causes would promulgate much-needed safety devices, improvements and legislation—advancements that continue to this day.

The first of the eighteen wrecks explored herein manifested in May 1853, when most of an express passenger train of the New York and New Haven Railroad careened through an open drawbridge at South Norwalk, Connecticut. Forty-six persons perished. The cause? The train's engineer failed to see or properly acknowledge a poorly located stop signal. The event remains the deadliest train disaster in the history of New England. Then, just a few months later, in August, a head-on collision occurred between two trains at Valley Falls, Rhode Island, on the Providence and Worcester Railroad, caused by one of the conductors not following company rules. Here, fourteen people died. It was also the first train wreck in America to be photographed.

Of the eighteen events explored in the pages ahead, nine took place in Massachusetts, while four unfolded in Connecticut. The state of Vermont experienced two of the disasters, while single events manifested in Rhode Island, New Hampshire and Maine. In all, the tragedies claimed the lives of nearly four hundred people.

In preparing this work, I have utilized railroad company records and annual reports, the annual reports of the various state railroad commissioners and the accident reports of the Interstate Commerce Commission, together with various newspapers, trade magazines and journal articles.

For their kind and generous help, I wish to thank Laura Smith, railroad archivist, Dodd Research Center, University of Connecticut; Andrea Rapacz, curator of collections, the Connecticut Historical Society; the Railway and Locomotive Historical Society; and J.W. Swanberg, Catherine Weller and Cliff Lund.

Images herein are from the Turner Railroad Collection at the Connecticut Historical Society in Hartford.

Readers desiring a greater understanding of train wrecks, accidents and disasters should consult the landmark book *Death Rode the Rails* by Mark Aldrich, along with a much earlier work, *Notes on Railroad Accidents* by Charles Francis Adams Jr. (see bibliography).

Lastly, owing to space limitations, it is not possible to include every extant fact about each of the train wrecks described herein. I respectfully ask for the reader's indulgence.

G.M.T.

CHAPTER 1

CONNECTICUT

SOUTH NORWALK, MAY 3, 1853

One can only imagine the sadness and grief that descended on this waterside community nearly 175 years ago. And why? Most of an express passenger train had careened through an open drawbridge that claimed the lives of forty-six persons and injured countless others. Not only did the event shock Connecticut residents and its legislature, but it also drew both sympathy and condemnation from citizens and publications all across America. Never had such a tragedy occurred, and it remains the deadliest railway disaster in New England's history.

It was on the New York and New Haven Railroad that the appalling disaster took place. Chartered in 1844 and fully opened five years later, its route largely traversed the saw-toothed coastline of Connecticut—from New Haven westward—to reach the New York setting of Williams Bridge in the Bronx. Here, it made a priceless connection with the New York and Harlem Railroad for New York City. Robert Schuyler, a wealthy and well-connected Harvard graduate, eventually became president of both railroads as well as the stock transfer agent of the former. In fact, "America's first railroad king" was at one time or another president of five different railroad companies, including the Illinois Central. After accruing a fortune with steamboats, he and his half brother George founded R. & G.L. Schuyler, a prominent railroad contracting and investment firm. Of Robert, more will be learned.[1]

The eventual success of the New York and New Haven would be premised on two factors: it was the last link built in the so-called Inland Route of rail lines connecting New York City with Boston (via New Haven, Hartford, Springfield and Worcester), and it intersected several prosperous north–south rail lines in Connecticut, which gave Schuyler's firm their New York City and western-bound traffic of freight, passengers, mail and express. Among the latter were the Housatonic, Naugatuck and Hartford and New Haven Railroads.

Professor Alexander Twining, a Yale graduate who studied engineering at West Point, surveyed two possible routes for the new line. His preferred one (and the one selected by the directors) often hugged the Connecticut shoreline with its numerous river crossings, marshlands, estuaries, hills and outcroppings of ledge and rock. Twining, however, did not receive the contract to build the line. Alfred Bishop—a noted canal and railroad builder who had built the Housatonic and Naugatuck entities—did. Robert Schuyler and Sidney Miller were also named in the construction contract, although the former eventually sold out to Bishop.

The compensation to Bishop and Miller—approximately $2.25 million—was partly paid with nearly $1 million of company stock. Interestingly, Bishop's lawyer son, William, also a Yale graduate, would take over his father's construction firm upon Alfred's early death and not only completed the New York and New Haven Railroad but also became its president. By using his powerful seat and persuasive powers in the Connecticut legislature, it was largely he who got the New York and New Haven consolidated, in 1872, with the Hartford and New Haven to form the legendary New York, New Haven and Hartford Railroad Company.

One clause of the aforementioned construction contract deserves note: "By the agreement with Bishop & Miller, they had the privilege of changing the location, under the approbation of the Chief Engineer, to improve the line and any expenditure thereby saved was for their benefit."[2] This privilege would eventually draw the wrath of the *American Railway Journal* on May 19, 1855: "The New York & New Haven Railroad was poorly built. The contractors did their own engineering and often to their interests. It has been stated that the curve in the road at South Norwalk was a change from the original location to save expenses. This curve, by concealing the drawbridge till eastbound trains were nearly upon it, was undoubtedly the cause of the fearful drawbridge disaster at that place." Henry Varnum Poor, the eminent railway investment guru and founder of *Poor's Manual of Railroads*, was the *Journal*'s editor and publisher.

The disaster at South Norwalk was not caused by faulty construction of the railroad's drawbridge over the Norwalk River. The heavily timbered and iron structure—a swing bridge that pivoted on a dedicated pier—measured 153 feet in length. When it was fully open, a horizontal clearance of 60 feet was created on each side of the pivot pier, allowing for the easy passage of vessels. At the time of the disaster, William Harford was the bridge tender. "By the regulations of the Company, it was his duty to open the draw for the passage of boats and vessels when they desired to pass, *without reference to the time when trains were due*."[3] (This mandate was in deference to the paramount rights of those engaged in navigation.) At high tide, the railway track on the bridge was approximately 25 feet above the water, the two channels having roughly a 9- to 12-foot depth. Below the "floor" of each channel there existed 10 to 15 feet of soft mud.

A tall wooden tower straddled the drawbridge at midpoint. From it, chains extended down to the bridge's two heavily timbered trusses, which aided their support. Mounted atop the tower was a forty-foot pole or mast having a rope and pulley. A two-foot metal ball—painted bright red but of late having aged to crimson—was attached to the rope to create a "ball signal." When the bridge tender hoisted the ball signal to the top of the mast, which was illuminated at night, this indicated to train engineers that the bridge was closed to marine traffic, and they could safely transit the drawbridge—hence the term "highball" or "O.K. to proceed." When the ball was in the down position, this meant the draw span was open for vessels and that an approaching train had to stop in advance of the movable span. Conflicting testimony would arise between the engineer of the wrecked train, who insisted the ball signal was up, while Harford and numerous witnesses insisted it was down.

When a bridge tender desired to open the drawbridge, he would first lower the ball signal to the bottom of the pole and place it on the floor of the bridge. No mechanical appliance or interlocking device existed to physically stop or derail a train should the ball signal in the down position be ignored. Subsequent investigation showed that the ball signal could first be seen by eastbound trains 3,312 feet from the draw. Thereafter, it could only be intermittently seen owing to tall trees, buildings and so on. Remarkably, the ball signal was largely obscured to engineers of eastbound trains while they rounded the aforementioned sharp curve.

To remind eastbound engineers of track switches near the South Norwalk station, a railway employee would wave a flag at approaching eastbound trains. Further, a special sign had been erected near the station warning engineers that a drawbridge lay ahead.[4] Further still, the following was printed in employee timetable No. 31, which became effective in February 1853: "All trains must run with care in approaching the Norwalk River Bridge. Trains going east from Norwalk Station will move around the curve with exceeding care. Conductors of trains out-of-time ('running late') are cautioned about crossing the bridge for they will be held responsible for the safety of their Trains." Finally, it was common knowledge that the South Norwalk drawbridge was frequently in the open position to accommodate the busy marine traffic.

The train that would careen into the Norwalk River was the railroad's eight o'clock morning express that ran between New York City and Boston via the Inland Route. That day, it consisted of a locomotive and tender, a baggage car, a second baggage car with a "smoking apartment" and five passenger cars. Approximately 218 passengers were aboard that spring day, many being eminent physicians who had just attended the sixth annual convention of the American Medical Association in the city. Having left somewhat late, the express had briefly stopped at Stamford for firewood and water, whereupon it resumed its easterly journey. It would make no stop at South Norwalk, which the express passed around 10:00 a.m.

The train's conductor, Charles Comstock, was, at the time of the disaster, in the second passenger car. Edward Tucker, the engineer, and fireman George Eisner were in the locomotive cab. A brakeman was also on the train whose duty it was to hand-crank (apply) the brakes to a car's wheels when commanded by the engineer—via the locomotive whistle—or when told to do so by Comstock. (Likely more than one brakeman was on the train, but just one is mentioned in news articles.) Tucker had lately returned to the company's employ, having been rehired by George Washington Whistler Jr., the railroad's superintendent and son of the famed American railway civil engineer. Tucker was still a spare engineer and not regularly assigned to the morning express. He had recently made three trips over the railroad between New York City and New Haven and knew firsthand of the company's five drawbridges in Connecticut—the longest being across the Housatonic River at Stratford-Devon.

In testimony, Tucker would claim that he began looking out of the locomotive cab for the South Norwalk drawbridge ball signal before reaching the station, the latter about one thousand feet from the drawbridge. He also testified that the ball signal he saw was in the up or all-clear position, allowing for his train to safely cross the drawbridge. Soon after passing South Norwalk station, the train entered the sharp curve, and the ball signal essentially vanished from his view.

About fifteen minutes before the tragedy, bridge tender Harford had lowered the ball signal and opened the movable span for the steamboat *Pacific*, in charge of Captain Joseph Byxbee, whereupon the vessel safely passed through the bridge's westerly opening. Upon starting to close the open span, Harford saw the morning express exiting the sharp curve and realized the inevitable. Tucker, in turn, could now see the open span and had about eleven seconds before his train would be at the abyss. After quickly applying the locomotive brake, he at once sounded the locomotive whistle for the brakeman to apply the manually operated car brakes. At no point in his testimony at the inquest did he state that he had closed the locomotive throttle or reversed the driving wheels—measures that would have greatly reduced the train's speed, estimated at twenty to twenty-five miles per hour.

Realizing his train was doomed, Tucker, his fireman and the brakeman jumped to the ground moments before the locomotive and tender shot across the sixty-foot-wide chasm and crashed into the abutment of the movable span. Both immediately sank, with the engine embedding itself into the thick mud below, the tender having flipped over atop the locomotive. After also hitting the pivot pier, the first baggage car fell into the dark waters and landed on the tender. Then came the combination baggage/smoking car, which eventually sank to the north side of the bridge. On top of the carnage there now descended the first passenger coach, its forward end crushing in as it struck the combination car. The second passenger car quickly followed and buried itself in the fragments of the first coach and its occupants. Miraculously, the impact of the crash splintered the third passenger coach; nearly half of it went down into the wreckage, while the remainder stayed on the track above. It was thought that some forty-five passengers in the first coach met instant death.[5]

Among the survivors in the splintered coach was Dr. Gurdon Wadsworth Russell, a graduate of Yale Medical School, whose vivid account of the disaster has become a classic. For many years, the distinguished physician would be employed as the medical director of the Aetna Life Insurance Company in Hartford. Like so many who survived the disaster, Russell would aid in the rescue operations of his fellow passengers.[6]

Tucker would incur serious injuries from his jump and would eventually be arrested for manslaughter. (Several witnesses wanted him lynched.) The baggage car master managed to escape through the car's broken roof, as did a newsboy. Conductor Comstock survived the disaster after making several attempts to wriggle through a broken car window. Most of the fatalities that day were caused by violent concussions and drownings. Many of the

THE LATE RAILWAY CALAMITY AT NORWALK, CONN.

This artist's conception of the South Norwalk tragedy appeared in the May 1853 issue of *Frank Leslie's Illustrated Newspaper*. Note signal pole and rope pulley above the tower at bridge's midpoint.

deceased were badly disfigured, their clothing torn, and certain victims could not be immediately identified. In all, about one hundred people were plunged into the Norwalk River.

Captain Byxbee of the steamboat had a boat lowered to rescue survivors, while several parties on land jumped into the river to aid those swimming to shore. Many of the survivors received first aid once on land. The bodies of the deceased were later brought to the station and placed in coffins that had been gratuitously supplied by the railroad company. Within two days, nearly two thousand persons were milling about the station identifying the dead, inquiring after survivors, visiting the wreck site or gathering luggage and personal belongings. Superintendent Whistler, in turn, wasted no time in bringing a large workforce to the site to salvage equipment and clear the wreckage so that train traffic could resume.

The coroner could not be found immediately after the disaster, so Justice John Weed of Fairfield County performed the necessary tasks. A jury of inquest was quickly formed with twelve jurors, who listened to testimony for several days from witnesses, which included railroad employees and officers.

Their written report appeared in full in the *New York Times* on May 11, 1853. The jury concluded that bridge tender Harford had done no wrong. "The immediate cause of this disaster was the negligence and recklessness of engineer Tucker."

However, the jury's report also stated that the entire responsibility for the disaster was not Tucker's alone but also on the railroad company and its management. To paraphrase its report: the ball signal was in a viewing position less than desirable; the ability to properly see the signal was intermittently obstructed for eastbound trains; the sharp curve preceding the bridge was poor engineering, as was the downgrade in the track between the station and the drawbridge; and having the drawbridge open when a train was possibly due was a deplorable policy. The next day, President Robert Schuyler had a lengthy article published in the *Times* titled "Notice to Stockholders" that defended the company's safety policies and essentially exonerated it from any guilt or fault.

Connecticut's General Assembly, then in session at Hartford and horrified over the disaster, quickly dispatched a Joint Select Committee to the wreck site to report back details. Legislation quickly evolved titled

SCENE AT THE DEPOT AFTER THE ACCIDENT—BRINGING IN THE BODIES.

The deceased, the injured and their luggage were brought to the station following the drawbridge calamity. Onlookers were numerous. Many of the fatalities were eminent physicians. Huge crowds gathered.

"An Act to Prevent Injuries and the Destruction of Life upon Railroads, and by Railroad Trains." Among its many measures, the act now required passenger trains to stop before crossing a drawbridge. Another section levied a $5,000 fine on any railroad company or its agents whose carelessness took the life of a passenger. (Schuyler's board eventually gave the families of victims a slightly larger largesse amounting to about $252,000 total, which forced the company to skip a stock dividend.) The act also formed a state railroad commission—the third one to be established in the United States—to oversee the operations and conduct of all the carriers. Its trio of commissioners, appointed by the General Assembly, were obligated to submit an annual report to the legislature about each railroad company, inspect each line annually or more, recommend improvements, investigate accidents and obtain and codify important financial information. Appended to their first report (in 1854) was a supplement detailing the disaster at South Norwalk.

Articles still appear about the horrendous disaster at South Norwalk, including ones suggesting that Tucker's locomotive and tender remain embedded in mud in the Norwalk River. Such, though, is not the case. Not long after the disaster, the *Hartford Courant* reported (on May 17, 1853) that both were raised and placed on the track by a powerful steam derrick brought in from New York. "The engine was but little broken."

And of Tucker himself? Approximately five years after the disaster, the engineer committed suicide.[7] And of Robert Schuyler, a supposed paragon of integrity and trust? One year after the drawbridge tragedy, it was discovered that the "first railroad king of America" had overissued and sold for his benefit some twenty thousand shares of New York and New Haven Railroad Company stock worth several million dollars—a misappropriation he had started before the South Norwalk disaster. The disgraced financier left the country, never was prosecuted and supposedly died in France or Italy; his body was eventually brought back to America for burial. After much litigation at the state and federal levels, the railroad company made good on the spurious shares.

TARIFFVILLE, JANUARY 15, 1878

Some twenty-five years after the South Norwalk tragedy, the next-deadliest railway disaster in Connecticut unfolded in the village of Tariffville, near

Simsbury. This is not to say that significant train wrecks failed to take place in the interim, for indeed many did. For example, two of note happened in 1865: one on the Housatonic Railroad (August 14) near Trumbull and the other on the Shore Line Railroad (October 15) at Rocky Neck in East Lyme. The former involved a "light" engine (pulling no cars) that telescoped into the rear of a passenger train; escaping steam from the locomotive scalded to death 8 passengers and injured 12. The latter involved a special eastbound train of 6 passenger cars carrying 275 wounded and sick Union soldiers. A broken rail caused it to derail in a deep rock cut (near today's Rocky Neck beach) that propelled the cars into a ghastly jumble. Sadly, 9 soldiers perished and 60 were injured.

In their 1879 annual report to the General Assembly, the railroad commissioners of Connecticut made the following statement: "In our last annual report we esteemed it a cause of congratulations that not one passenger out of *nearly ninety-five million* carried over the roads of this State during the preceding ten years, had been killed by causes beyond their control. We regret that we cannot make a similar record for the year just closed."[8] The commissioners were, of course, referring to the excursion train that broke through the west span of the truss bridge over the Farmington River at Tariffville, on the Connecticut Western Railroad, which caused the deaths of thirteen persons and injured seventy others.

According to author Stewart Holbrook, the Tariffville disaster sorely tried the faith of many devout Yankee Christians. "This was because the wreck occurred to an excursion train that was returning to their homes in Connecticut towns more than a thousand earnest pilgrims who had been to hear the great evangelist Dwight L. Moody and his songster, Ira D. Sankey, perform at Hartford."[9] After the revival meeting broke up at the old skating rink near Bushnell Park, waiting at the Hartford terminal of the Connecticut Western was a ten-car train with two locomotives that would deliver attendees to their homes in such settings as Bloomfield, Tariffville, Winsted, Norfolk, Canaan and Salisbury.

When every car was full, Conductor Thomas Elmore gave the "highball" signal around 9:15 p.m. Shortly after 10:00 p.m., the heavy train, which was also pulling two freight cabooses, reached the Tariffville bridge that spanned the Farmington River. "It was not a new bridge," notes Holbrook, "and Elmore, if nobody else, had thought it rather shaky when the special had crossed it that afternoon on the way to Hartford. Shaky it must have been, for the two locomotives had arrived little more on the furthermost span before it started to give way, at first a slow and sickening collapse, followed by an instant later by a tremendous crash. Both locomotives went down onto and through the ice of the river, dragging four coaches [one a baggage car] after them."[10] After an eerie silence, chaos followed.

The sixty-six-mile Connecticut Western opened between Hartford and the northwestern corner of the state in December 1871. By leasing a tiny portion of a New York railroad, the company reached Millerton, New York, and connections were made to the Hudson River. Egbert Butler, a prominent banker from Norfolk, had been the company's prime mover. Among the firm's other key players was former Connecticut governor Alexander Hamilton Holley of Salisbury and William Barnum of Lime Rock, a wealthy industrialist, United States senator and chairman of the Democratic National Committee who became the railroad's president.

In the year of the Tariffville disaster, revenues of Connecticut Western tallied $227,704, while net earnings amounted to $52,684. Its overall finances were not good, and bondholders were anxious about unpaid interest. That year, the railroad owned ten locomotives and eleven passenger coaches. Several stiff grades and sharp curves peppered its east–west route, for the track had to overcome many north–south hills. Of its twenty-seven stations in Connecticut, no fewer than four were situated in Norfolk, where "Summit" had the highest elevation of any in the state—1,333 feet above tidewater. To complete its route, an imposing viaduct had to be built over the Whiting River and a road in East Canaan along with two substantial bridges over the Farmington River: one at Tariffville, another at Satan's Kingdom in New Hartford.[11]

After departing Hartford, the Moody excursion train made a brief stop in Bloomfield, where six boys from New Hartford climbed aboard between the baggage car and first coach for a free ride home. Then, a stop was made at Tariffville, which a period guidebook described as "a village situated on an eminence commanding a beautiful view of the Farmington River and valley." Here, the locomotive tenders were topped off with water. George Hatch was the engineer of the first locomotive, named *Salisbury*; Thomas Franey was at the controls of *Tariffville*, the second engine. During the journey from Hartford, passengers sang gospel revival songs.

About a half mile beyond Tariffville station, the train slowed to around eight miles an hour to cross the two Howe truss bridges and trestlework over the Farmington River. Each of the spans measured 163 feet in length and was about 10 feet above the river, which flowed to the north. Constructed of heavy wooden timbers and iron suspension rods, the bridge was erected in 1870 by the A.D. Briggs & Company of Springfield, Massachusetts. After safely crossing the eastern span, engineers Hatch and Franey began inching their train across the westerly span.

But just as the lead locomotive came off the latter and began negotiating trestlework leading to land, the westerly span started to give way—at first a slow and sickening collapse, followed an instant later by a tremendous crash. Both trusses of the span, along with the two locomotives and baggage car, immediately fell together toward the south, the forward engine overturning, the second one landing on the ground just behind it, followed by the baggage car. "Three passenger cars on the east span were now forced into the opening by the momentum of the train behind them, the first one being turned to a position at right angles with the bridge and the second and third with their ends in the river and their rear platforms against the center pier, whereupon two slipped fully into the river. The remaining six cars of the train remained undamaged."[12]

The sound of splintering timbers and cries of agony filled the cold night air. Within moments, escape and rescue efforts began while frigid water started to fill the submerged cars. Many passengers inside the first coach would perish owing to blunt trauma and drowning. Others in the remaining cars managed to escape through broken car roofs and windows. Severely injured survivors, once extracted, were removed from the wreckage and placed on the five-inch-thick ice, then hauled to land on improvised wood sleds made from the wreckage.

Riding the train that night was railroad superintendent John Jones, who ran back to the Tariffville station to summon help. His first telegraphic message went to company offices in West Winsted: "Send extra train with surgeons and Mr. Greer. Three cars through the bridge at Tariffville."[13] (Greer was the railroad's roadmaster.) Within an hour, a relief train was en route from West Winsted with doctors, medical supplies and railroad workers with tools. Following this, Jones telegraphed assistant superintendent John McManus in Hartford on the Hartford, Providence and Fishkill Railroad and asked for another "train of mercy," as the Hartford office of the Connecticut Western had closed after the revival train had left.

By one o'clock the next morning, the requested train had left Hartford. The dozen or so doctors on board had been summoned by Dr. D.P. Pelletier, who, after being contacted by McManus, dashed to the Capitol Avenue Drug Store in Hartford to use their telephone; this was thought to be the first emergency telephone call made in America. Meanwhile, church and factory bells were rung in Tariffville to awaken residents, many of whom opened their homes to the wounded. The well-known Thurston House Hotel threw open its doors as well. Before long, the little telegraph office inside the station became besieged by railroad men, passengers and, later, reporters. The young operator became overwhelmed with the mass of dispatches.

Once the relief train from West Winsted arrived, the doctors got off and went about attending to the wounded, while railway workers axed and sawed their way into the coaches looking for survivors. Similar scenes unfolded once the relief train from Hartford arrived. Around 3:00 a.m., the latter made a return trip to Hartford with deceased and wounded passengers. "The heads of many were wrapped in bandages; arms were suspended in slings. Several of the fatalities were women and handkerchiefs covered their faces—the pallor of death had changed their features to something horrible to view."[14] Railroad president Caleb Camp, also aboard the special that night, rode the train of mercy back to Hartford and went about consoling survivors. After its arrival, the train departed to Plainville on Fishkill rails and then was switched north to New Hartford, where it intersected the Connecticut Western. Sadly, most of the boys from New Hartford—hoping for a free ride home—drowned. Engineer George Hatch, also of New Hartford, had been badly scalded by escaping steam. He was rescued from the river but died the next day.

Hundreds of spectators eventually swarmed the wreck site in the days ahead, with many taking home wood and iron fragments as souvenirs. Among those inspecting the site for how the disaster occurred were Connecticut's three railroad commissioners: George Woodruff of Litchfield, John Bacon of Danbury and George Arnold of Haddam. Railroad men from other companies also combed the wreckage, as did bridge specialists. Whereas differing opinions circulated as to how the span collapsed—from rotten bridge timbers to excessive weight, from running a train with two engines to the lead engine first derailing—increased attention was drawn to the iron suspension rods that were forged to hold up the bridge. Remains of the latter were sent out for scientific testing.

A jury of inquest with twelve jurors was soon impaneled by the coroner to investigate the wreck's cause and who was responsible. Starting on January 22, they heard testimony from passengers, railway employees and company officers, along with bridge builders, bridge experts and civil engineers. The hearings, held in the Thurston House Hotel, ended on February 13. In the audience were Connecticut's three railroad commissioners, who decided not to hold their own investigation. Mansfield Merriman, a civil engineer instructor at the Sheffield Scientific School at Yale College, not only appeared as a witness but also wrote an assessment of the disaster to the editor of the *Hartford Daily Courant*, and the paper published it on the first day

Once on trestlework, the engine *Salisbury* of the Connecticut Western Railroad flipped over into the Farmington River. Its engineer, scalded and trapped underneath, was rescued but later died.

of the inquest. In it, Merriman—a native of Southington, Connecticut—made a point of chastising the railroad commissioners as far as bridge inspections were concerned, as they did not possess the proper engineering knowledge or background to determine if a bridge was truly in a safe, sound condition. Not only did the *Courant* give excellent coverage of the disaster, but it reported on each daily session of the inquest as well.

In the end, the jury could not render a unanimous verdict as to what caused the disaster or who was to blame. Eight of the jurors were convinced that the train's conductor and his fellow employees along with Superintendent Jones were not responsible for what happened. Further, there was no evidence that the bridge had been tampered with to wreck the train, nor was there sufficient evidence that any derailment of engines or cars occurred and that placing a second engine on the train was not censurable.

The majority of jurors also declared in their report that certain materials of the bridge had become deteriorated, to wit: that the iron suspension rods (from being overstrained or from some other cause) had lost their tensile and sustaining power and that the timber of the chords (from many years exposure to the elements without covering or paint) had become weakened by decay to such an extent as to render the bridge unsafe and unfit for the purpose for which it was constructed, thereby rendering it dangerously

Three passenger cars are in the Farmington River at different angles. In the immediate foreground is the fourth: a baggage car. Nearby, men are balancing themselves on bridge timbers. The view looks toward Tariffville.

weak and defective. Lastly, the majority "finds that the responsibility of the sad disaster largely rests upon the directors of the Connecticut Western Railroad Company, that they are deserving of censure for allowing the use of the bridge after its materials had become defective to the point of danger, and for permitting so many years to pass without covering, strengthening, and protecting same, in such a manner as not to jeopardize human life."[15]

The four jurors in the minority claimed the bridge was indeed in a safe condition for trains to pass regardless if it had one or more locomotives; that the wooden construction materials of the bridge were not really in a deteriorated condition by exposure to the elements; and that the iron suspension rods had not been overstrained sufficiently to cause any weakening or danger. They were convinced, however, that a derailment had occurred before the engines and cars toppled over that caused a shock sufficient to cause the structure to fail. (It was rumored that all four jurors were stockholders in the Connecticut Western Railroad Company.)

A quotation by the Connecticut railroad commissioners opened our story of the Tariffville disaster. Also within their 1879 report was extensive mathematical and engineering data regarding the defective iron suspension rods. But it was George Vose, a professor of civil engineering at Bowdoin College and later the Massachusetts Institute of Technology, who perhaps best summarized the calamity:

> *The Tariffville bridge, like most structures of this kind, relied entirely upon iron rods to keep the woodwork together. Although the rods were too small and seriously defective in manufacture, the bridge ought not to have fallen from that cause. When we look at the quality of the iron, we have the cause of the fall. The fracture of the tested rods showed a very inferior quality of metal. The rods broke in the bridge exactly where we should look for the failure, viz. in the screw threads at the end. No ordinary inspection would have detected this weakness. No inspection did detect it, but a proper specification faithfully carried out would have prevented the disaster.*[16]

The wreck site at Tariffville was eventually cleared, the collapsed truss was rebuilt and train schedules resumed, despite the company's financial condition continuing to worsen. Cash settlements to the families of the victims—perhaps $300 to $700 for each—could hardly be afforded. Before long, unpaid interest on bonds forced bondholders to foreclose and have the company reorganized as the Hartford and Connecticut Western Railroad. The bondholders of old converted their securities into preferred stock of the new firm. As was so often the case, common stockholders of the old firm went to the wall.

A small wonder that following the Tariffville disaster, the railroad commissioners required all railroad companies in the state to thoroughly inspect their wooden bridges having iron suspension rods and—if they were suspect—reinforce or replace them with ones having superior strength.

Trains no longer come and go in Tariffville, thanks largely to the automobile and truck. It is even difficult to locate where the ill-fated Farmington River bridge of the Connecticut Western once stood. Nevertheless, devotees still cherish the company's memory—better known in its final years as the Central New England Railway. Many of them revel in walking on or hunting for its largely abandoned right of way west of Tariffville, especially in the beautiful rolling hills of Litchfield County.

BRIDGEPORT, JULY 11, 1911

This train wreck was actually one of eighteen that occurred on the New York, New Haven and Hartford Railroad (the "New Haven") between 1911 and 1913. The extraordinary series, superbly written about by historian Mark Aldrich, were chiefly caused by derailments, collisions and rear-ending scenarios. Some fifty passengers were killed between those years, twenty railway employees died and nearly three hundred persons were injured.[17]

Fourteen of the above wrecks would occur in Connecticut, the remainder in Massachusetts. The first took place at Fairfield, Connecticut, and involved four separate trains; the only other wreck in New England involving that many had previously occurred (on a different company) at East Thompson, Connecticut, in 1891. Two of the eighteen would claim more than a dozen lives: Bridgeport, Connecticut (the second one to occur and the subject of this sub-chapter), and the last one at North Haven, Connecticut, the subject of our next story. The total loss of lives, the injuries, the huge amount of destruction and the negative publicity surrounding each event hardly endeared the New Haven Railroad to the public or train travelers.

The disaster at Bridgeport involved but a single train: the *Federal Express*, denoted in the New Haven timetable as No. 72. Jointly operated with the Pennsylvania Railroad, it ran between Washington, D.C., and Boston. The private business car of United States president William Howard Taft was often attached to it whenever the country's chief executive came to New England.

The northbound edition of No. 72 was made up in the Washington, D.C. yards of the Pennsylvania Railroad. On July 10, it departed the nation's capital at 5:35 p.m. with a locomotive and tender, a special car belonging to the Department of Commerce and Labor Fish Commission, a Pennsylvania Railroad baggage car, a day coach belonging to the New Haven and six Pullman sleeping cars—some accommodating players of the St. Louis Cardinals baseball team and their manager. (The team was to play the Boston Braves the following day.) Many southern people filled the other Pullmans trying to escape that summer's blistering heat.

Upon reaching the sprawling Jersey City terminal of the Pennsylvania, the Federal Express was disassembled, and its cars were shuttled aboard a huge car float and ferried around the southern end of Manhattan, by powerful tugboats, to the Harlem River terminal of the New Haven Railroad located in the Bronx. The train was then reassembled and a fresh locomotive and tender, belonging to the New Haven, were attached. In the cab now were engineer Arthur Curtis and fireman Walter Ryan. Just as the train started to move at 1:52 a.m., the yardmaster reminded Curtis that the fish car it was hauling had to be dropped off in Bridgeport proper and that the crossover switches and signals there, enabling his train to move from express track No. 2 to local track No. 4, would be lined for him before he arrived. The train left the Bronx fifty-seven minutes late, which no doubt frustrated Curtis, who had a reputation on the railroad for running on time. (The engineer had recently returned to work owing to a serious bout with measles.) The Express would make eleven stops that early morning before reaching Bridgeport.

At New Rochelle, New York, No. 72 entered the impressively maintained, four-track mainline of the New Haven, which was ballasted with crushed rock and substantial steel rails. Crossovers were installed along the route to New Haven that permitted trains to be switched (by operators in signal towers) to different tracks, as traffic demanded. The signal system consisted of "distant" and "home" semaphore signals, along with low-to-the-ground "dwarf" signals that governed movements through crossover switches. Operators within the signal towers manipulated the switches and signals usually per directives from the train dispatcher.[18]

Between the various station stops, Curtis ran to New Haven at maximum speed unless subject to speed restrictions. Because of his late departure, making up time no doubt concerned him. Although he had lately recovered from the measles, there exists no record of him taking medications that could have made him drowsy or impaired his vision, memory or thinking. Overall, he was well regarded by his fellow workers and his employer and strived to run his trains on time.

Several months before the disaster, the railroad company had been straightening its roadbed as it entered Bridgeport. Its four-track mainline was elevated above street level beginning at the western line of the city until well within the heart of the busy metropolis. Its four tracks sat on an earthen embankment "walled up on each side by great, rough-hewn grey granite blocks except where streets passed under the embankment."[19] Such gaps were bridged by massive steel trusses. The impending disaster occurred at such a gap called Fairfield Avenue, the second-most important thoroughfare in the city. It was some eighteen feet high and could even admit streetcars and trolley poles.

Near where the four tracks crossed Fairfield Avenue there stood the Burr Road signal tower, a slender, drab-colored structure about three stories tall, and in front of this building are the switches by which trains cross over from track to track. Fully expecting the Federal Express, the tower operator, per directives from the train dispatcher, had all necessary signals and crossover switches properly aligned so the train could cross from track numbers two to four to set off the fish car in Bridgeport. (The Burr Road signal tower was about one and a half miles west of the station.) Per the railroad's rulebook, trains about to encounter the kind of "double-slip crossover switches" Curtis was about to negotiate had to reduce their speed to fifteen miles per hour.[20]

The Federal Express was normally due at Bridgeport station at 2:18 a.m. but this morning was estimated to arrive at 3:38 a.m. For whatever reason, the train roared into the Burr Road interlocking limits, disregarded the restricting distant and home signal indications and at 3:32 a.m. dashed through the double slip crossover switches at between fifty-five and sixty miles per hour. The train immediately derailed except for the last two Pullman cars and then proceeded to destroy the south girder of the eighty-five-foot steel span that crossed Fairfield Avenue. It then ran along the ties and ground, overturned and dove down the embankment into the street below. The locomotive lay more than four hundred feet from the point of derailment. Whether Curtis was conscious as the disaster unfolded remains conjecture.

As noted, thirteen persons died in the Bridgeport disaster, and among those who perished were Curtis and his fireman. Most of the passenger fatalities occurred in the wooden day coach, which was reduced to splinters. The baseball players, largely unharmed, swung into action and performed many heroic rescues. (Their game that day with the Boston Braves would

Cars of the wrecked Federal Express lay in Fairfield Avenue in Bridgeport. Why its engineer roared through nearby crossover switches at fifty-five miles per hour—instead of fifteen—will never be known.

Cleaning up the wreck site at Bridgeport. Track laborers, *at left*, are laying down new crossties and rails. Afterward, the distant wrecking crane will get closer to raise up fallen cars and debris.

be canceled.) Bridgeport fire, police and medical personnel sped to the scene and aided those in distress, and staffers of three hospitals attended the injured. The railroad company itself wasted little time in dispatching track workers and wreck equipment to clean up the site.

The New Haven Railroad and several government agencies investigated the wreck: all blamed engineer Curtis for the disaster. The coroner and government investigators additionally cited the railroad for installing a complex crossover in such a tight location—one that forced trains not to exceed fifteen miles per hour. The Interstate Commerce Commission investigator stated in his report that if "number 18 or 20 double slip crossover switches" had been installed instead of a number 8, the accident would not have happened.

We close with the thoughts of engineer Curtis's widow. She was interviewed by a local newspaper reporter at the family's home in the Bronx, where three little children were now fatherless. She insisted:

> *"It was overwork that killed my poor husband. For eight hours on Monday, my husband ran a switch engine about the freight yard in the Bronx. You know how hot it was in the heat of the day. He came home to me and the*

babies, and we just rested about the house in the early evening, gasping for some fresh air.

"Around nine o'clock that evening, the call came for Arthur to report for duty as engineer of the Federal Express, which was to leave about midnight. Tired as he was the poor fellow braced up at once, for that call meant some extra money for us, and we needed the money. My husband had just recovered from a three week illness. He was sick with measles, and we were quarantined. Our income was cut off and we used up our savings. My husband, although employed by New York, New Haven & Hartford for more than thirteen years, eleven of them as an engineer, never got a regular run. He was always careful and occasionally he had taken the Federal Express out before. I am sure he knew every turn in the road, and I cannot understand how he could do wrong unless the tired feelings were too much for him. He had complained during the evening of being very weak from the extreme heat of Monday."

A railroad company clerk was eventually sent out to notify Mrs. Curtis of her husband's death, but merely told her there had been a wreck. She wandered around the Bronx for two hours seeking any word about her husband before a kind trainman took her aside and told her the truth. She collapsed and was taken home.[21]

NORTH HAVEN, SEPTEMBER 2, 1913

Of the eighteen wrecks on the New Haven Railroad referenced in the previous story, the deadliest—certainly one of the saddest—occurred immediately after Labor Day 1913 at North Haven, Connecticut. It claimed the lives of twenty-one persons and seriously injured forty. The disaster involved two summer-only passenger trains that were patronized by the monied class. In brief, the famed Bar Harbor Express, while at a standstill having just passed a red stop signal, was rear-ended by the White Mountain Express. In a twist of fate, the wreck took place on the first working day of Howard Elliot, the railroad's new president, who replaced the controversial Charles Sanger Mellen. Incredibly, just two hours before the horrifying event, Elliot had passed through North Haven, by train, en route from his summer home in New Hampshire to New Haven. As one party presciently remarked, his arrival was "a baptism by fire."

Owing to heavy holiday traffic that Labor Day, the Bar Harbor Express—train No. 91 in the New Haven Railroad timetable—was run in two sections:

first 91 and second 91, the latter being involved in the North Haven tragedy. Composed largely of sleeping cars gathered from various points in southern Maine on the Maine Central Railroad, second 91 departed Mount Desert Ferry station at 3:40 p.m. Its journey to New York City, involving several railroads, was made via Portland, Worcester, Springfield, Hartford, North Haven and New Haven. In addition to having a locomotive and tender, the train that holiday had a Maine Central baggage car and ten wooden sleeping cars, half of which had been built in the 1890s. The train was delivered by the Boston and Albany Railroad to Springfield, Massachusetts, where a New Haven locomotive and tender were then placed on the point in charge with engineer Rufus Wands in charge. His fireman that early morning was John Mahoney. Brace Adams was the train's conductor.[22]

The White Mountain Express of the Boston and Maine Railroad originated at various points in the picturesque White Mountains. Because of holiday traffic, it, too, would run that Labor Day in two sections: first 95 and second 95. The first section, which played into the North Haven disaster, left Bretton Woods, New Hampshire, for New York City at 9:00 p.m. It consisted of an engine and tender, a baggage car, a coach car and five wooden sleeping cars. It was delivered by the Boston and Maine to the New Haven Railroad at Springfield, where the B&M locomotive and tender were taken off and replaced with New Haven motive power. The new engineer, Augustus Miller, was joined in the locomotive cab by fireman Elbert Robertson. Conductor Fowler rode in the coach car.

The third district of New Haven's Shore Line Division (later called the Hartford Division) was sixty-two miles long and stretched between New Haven and Springfield via North Haven, Wallingford, Meriden, Hartford and Windsor. Composed of two mainline tracks—one for northbound traffic, another for southbound trains—it ran straight as an arrow for about two miles north of the wreck site in North Haven. Trains were operated in the district by train orders and timetable authority and were spaced apart by automatic enclosed disk block signals known as "banjo signals," as they resembled the musical instrument inverted. The banjo system in the district was about twenty-five years old and was slowly being replaced with automatic semaphore signals.

The signal mast that supported a banjo signal was twenty feet high, the masts being spaced about one mile apart between New Haven and Springfield. (The space between two banjo signal masts was called a "block.") At night, the signal's illuminated lamp could display either a green light to proceed or a red light to stop. (A red signal meant there was a train in the next block.) Locomotive engineers were required to bring their trains to a full stop just before a red signal, after which they could cautiously proceed to the next signal *if the track immediately ahead was known to be clear*. Engineers would be held responsible for any accident that might occur to their train that was proceeding under such circumstances.

Another factor playing a key role in the North Haven disaster was Rule 99 in the New Haven Railroad's rulebook for train employees. It specifically stated that when a train was stopped or delayed and might be overtaken by another train, a flagman had to be immediately sent out from the rear of the train with danger signals for a sufficient distance to ensure full protection from being rear-ended. The danger signals at night included a red lamp, red-fire fusees and a supply of warning torpedoes—the latter being strapped to the rails and causing a loud explosion when run over by a locomotive. According to Rule 99, the flagman had to place the first set of torpedoes twelve telegraph poles or 1,992 feet (12 x 166 = 1,992) from the train's rear and fasten another set on the rails four telegraph poles beyond. He then had to wait to stop any approaching train, unless recalled by the locomotive whistle, in which case he was to leave a lighted red fusee between the rails.

According to the investigation report of the Interstate Commerce Commission, second No. 91 of the Bar Harbor Express left Springfield on Tuesday morning, September 2, at 5:13 a.m. A heavy fog enveloped the Connecticut countryside. The train passed Wallingford—about three and a half miles north of the wreck site—at 6:43 a.m. Five minutes later, engineer Wands slightly overran signal number 23 (one and a half miles north of North Haven station), which was displaying red, as another train was in the block ahead.

Wands claimed in testimony that his vision in the fog was limited to several hundred feet, thus he did not see the red signal until close to it, whereupon he applied the emergency train brake. After stopping, flagman Charles Murray got off the Bar Harbor Express and started to walk back with his danger signals to stop any following train. (Investigations revealed he did not go back far enough; he merely went two telegraph poles instead of twelve.) After a delay of several minutes on account of releasing the air brakes and rebuilding air pressure, the train cautiously started ahead, but without Murray. It moved about one car length and again stopped upon being signaled to do so by conductor Adams. The latter told Wands to sound the whistle signal for Murray to return to the train, which he did. While waiting for the flagman to return, the White Mountain Express—weighing some 1.2 million pounds and supposedly moving at forty miles per hour—plowed into the rear of the Bar Harbor Express.

The White Mountain Express—known that Labor Day as first No. 95—had departed Springfield at 5:33 a.m. The heavy fog in Connecticut had not lifted. The train passed Meriden at 6:44 and Wallingford at 6:51 a.m. Suddenly, just north of the wreck site, engineer Miller heard several torpedoes explode and immediately saw the red rear marker lights on the last sleeping car of the Bar Harbor Express and then a red banjo signal. In an instant, Miller realized that something terrible was about to occur. He quickly applied the train's emergency brake, reversed the engine's driving wheels and, with his fireman, safely jumped to the ground. The violent rear-end collision that followed (about 6:55 a.m.) destroyed the Bar Harbor's two rear sleeping cars, turned the third sleeper (Chisholm) on its side and derailed the rear of the fourth sleeper. After smashing into the cars, the nose of Miller's engine was reportedly nearly vertical.

After the collision, an eerie silence briefly fell upon the carnage. Then, several sleeping car passengers, who had escaped the wreck, began to wander about the site in their bedclothes. Other passengers inside the sleepers, however, were either dead, writhing in pain or crying for help. Some were pinned under heavy timber planks and iron; others were outright mangled. "The two rear Pullmans loaded with sleeping tourists were broken into bits, scarcely one of which was no more than a four-foot square; passengers were

The mangled engine of the White Mountain Express after smashing into the Bar Harbor Express in North Haven. The view looks toward Wallingford and Hartford.

hurled high and far beside the track, the dead amid the dying in the nearby green melon field."[23] A young female passenger in the last sleeper was flung atop Miller's locomotive in her nightdress, bleeding and scorched. In fact, the big, Pacific-type locomotive was partially covered with bedding, clothes and personal belongings. In sleeper car Kesota, nineteen passengers were instantly crushed to death. Fortunately, fires did not break out. On nearby telegraph pole wires were strewn clothes, blankets, sheets, pillows and even men's neck ties.

Sixty-five boy campers, two of whom perished, were in Chisholm, the overturned sleeper. They were returning home with their teachers from Camp Cobbossee in Monmouth, Maine, which is still in existence in 2024. Thirty-five of the boys held certificates from the U.S. Life-Saving Corp and, once escaping the overturned car, did outstanding work helping the injured. In another sleeper, unharmed, were forty young girls from the upscale Sidwell Friends School in Washington, D.C. They were returning home from a summer camp at Maine's Belgrade Lakes.

The wreck in North Haven occurred in a sparsely populated area near what was then called Miller's Crossing. Hearing the trains crash was Peter Miller, a lithographer, who lived near the railroad and was tending his garden. He immediately dashed to the wreck site and aided in rescue efforts. His house had a telephone, and soon emergency calls were summoning police, ambulances, doctors and railroad company headquarters in New Haven. A trolley car line and a road (today state Route 5) were also near the crash site. At 7:20 a.m., a southbound trolley from Wallingford ground to a halt when its motorman spotted the carnage. The few passengers aboard jumped out to also aid those in distress. Mattresses and blankets about the wreckage were collected and placed inside the trolley, and the initial group of fatalities was rushed to the trolley car barn on James Street in New Haven. Here they were placed on cots until the bodies could be identified. One young woman, mangled in the wreck, was identified by a Yale pin she was wearing, given to her by her fiancé. A special train from Hartford, with twelve doctors and railroad workers with emergency tools, soon arrived at North Haven, as did a squad of police officers from New Haven. Crowds of onlookers were quick to gather.

Railroad officials soon appeared in North Haven, as did an investigator from the Connecticut Public Utilities Commission in Hartford and personnel from the Interstate Commerce Commission in Washington, D.C. The coroner of New Haven County, Eli Mix, appeared too; he conducted that day a secret hearing with the employees of the two trains at the railroad's

Media coverage of the terrible rear-end collision in North Haven seemed never-ending. Enormous crowds gathered day after day to view the carnage. Some even pocketed little souvenirs.

offices in New Haven. A formal inquest, also conducted by the coroner, began the following day at the county courthouse in New Haven, again in private, but a transcript was eventually given out to the press. At the behest of Mix, engineer Miller was arrested for criminal negligence along with flagman Murray. Both posted bonds. The Connecticut Public Utilities Commission investigator also had conductor Adams charged for not showing sufficient interest in the safety of his train and knowing a train was closely following his Bar Harbor Express. Among the railroad officials subpoenaed for the various investigations were General Manager Bardo, Signal Engineer Morrison and General Superintendent Woodward. Howard Elliot, the railroad's new president, who did not come to the wreck site, oversaw operational details from his New Haven office.

Wreck crews from the railroad soon appeared at the site and began the arduous job of cleaning up the disaster and making repairs to the track. Among the personnel from the Interstate Commerce Commission appearing were Hiram Belnap, its chief safety appliance investigator, and the commission's chairman, Charles McChord, who would author that agency's exhaustive investigation report, which can be read online.[24]

The railroad and the government agencies all blamed engineer Miller for having caused the North Haven disaster; they claimed he was going too fast for the foggy conditions and failed to stop his train before a red banjo signal. Also at fault was flagman Murray of the Bar Harbor Express, who did not go back far enough to stop Miller's train. The agencies also censured the railroad company for not having a modern signal system fully in place and for still employing wooden sleeping cars. President Elliot repeatedly informed the press and public that changes and improvements to operating policies would be made, that the signal system upgrade to automatic semaphores (then in progress) would be rapidly completed and that existing steel sleeping car orders with the Pullman Company would be expedited.

Two asides: the crowds viewing the North Haven wreckage grew to twenty thousand persons, and many were observed combing the wreckage for loot. Eventually, however, ropes were stretched parallel to the tracks, and with the aid of "big sticks," the police kept the public at a distance. As if the air of a holiday picnic prevailed, vendors of popcorn, peanuts and beverages set up shop on the road near the wreck and proceeded to do a brisk business.

On a more serious note:

> *U.S. President Woodrow Wilson passed by the wreckage at 9:50 tonight* [September 3] *en route from Cornish, New Hampshire to Washington,*

D.C. His train was more than an hour late, but the Federal Express was held for the connection in New Haven. The President's train was taken over the same route where earlier in the day the disastrous wreck of the Bar Harbor Express occurred. The President stood on the observation platform and saw the wreckage as it was being burned. The fires gleamed in the dark as the train moved slowly by.[25]

CHAPTER 2

RHODE ISLAND

VALLEY FALLS, AUGUST 12, 1853

A considerable amount of railroad history unfolded in America during the 1850s. Among the landmark events were the construction of many new rail lines, the quest for faster train speeds, technological improvements and—unfortunately—a profound number of accidents and wrecks. The second-deadliest railroad disaster to occur in New England unfolded in 1853, at Valley Falls, Rhode Island. Fourteen persons died in the wreckage, and forty were seriously injured.

The wreck at Valley Falls took place on the Providence and Worcester Railroad, regarded as one of the better-built and operated firms in New England. The company was chartered in 1844 and opened three years later. Its forty-three-mile route frequently followed the Blackstone River and the Blackstone Canal; the railroad had purchased the latter and its towpath. Its single-track route, which had numerous stations and passing tracks, served many industrial communities, such as Whitinsville, Uxbridge, Woonsocket and Lonsdale. Below Central Falls, until it built its own track to Providence, the company shared the one belonging to the Boston and Providence Railroad.

In brief, the disaster involved the head-on collision of two scheduled passenger trains: a "down" or southbound train en route to Providence, Rhode Island, and an "up" or northbound train proceeding from that state capital to Worcester. Because of reduced fares in effect that summer day, the down train was conveying about four hundred excursionists in eight cars, largely factory operatives (workers) who, for the most part, were looking forward to a day's outing on inviting Narragansett Bay and breathing the invigorating salt air.

One of the more prominent newspapers proceeded to describe the fateful collision in a somewhat Victorian tone: "Disagreeable necessity obliges us to shock the sensibilities of our readers, by the recital of yet another terrible calamity from a collision of Railway trains." According to the article, the excursion or down train was "out of time" (running late) and proceeding at about forty miles per hour. The two trains met at a sharp curve below the Valley Falls station. "The spectacle presented was most horrible. The wreck of the engines, both of which were demolished, and the killed and the wounded all lay together in one unsightly mess."[26]

That newspaper's Rhode Island correspondent went on to say:

> *The cars of the down train suffered most. Several were broken into pieces, and two of them were run together as you would close a spy-glass. The up train received but little damage; no persons in it were killed or seriously injured. The excursion train consisted of six long passenger cars, densely crowded, and the cries of those who were within, and who were not instantly killed, were heart-rending. As they were taken out, some with broken arms and some with limbs and bodies otherwise mangled, the painfulness of the scene presented cannot be described. For a time, an intense excitement prevailed, and imprecations were hurled at the heads of railroad companies, directors, conductors, engineers, and all who are in any way connected with railroads.*[27]

The first passenger car of the excursion train, located behind the engine and its tender, contained about sixty passengers, nearly all from Whitinsville, from whence the train departed at 6:25 a.m. Many inside that car were killed or wounded. The third passenger car was driven over some twenty feet into the second car, crushing everything within. The deceased and injured had to be dragged out from beneath. Thousands of people visited the wreck site during the day to see the bodies of those who perished and the ruins of the cars and engines.

An inquest was convened to determine who caused the blunder and to bring charges; it was conducted at the town hall in Valley Falls before coroner George Dana. Six jurors were impaneled, and numerous parties rendered sworn—sometimes conflicting—testimony. The inquest was conducted in private, as the bodies of the deceased were still in the hall and an excited crowd outside had to be kept at bay. According to Ephriam Gates, the excursion train's engineer, his train arrived at Valley Falls at 7:32 a.m. (Station master Jonathan Chace claimed it was 7:36.) Frederick Putnam, the train's conductor, told Gates at the Falls that he had four minutes to reach Boston Switch, where they were to meet the up train from Providence. (The latter was pulling two coaches and due at Boston Switch at 7:32.) By company rules, the latter had to wait for any overdue down train a full five minutes, and if it did not appear, the journey could resume.

Gates told Putnam that he could make Boston Switch before the up train could technically depart at 7:37—if it was on time. (Chace and others claimed in testimony he could not.) The down train then departed Valley Falls. The two trains collided head on less than a half mile below the Valley Falls station. Just before the collision, Gates had reversed his engine and sounded the whistle for the brakeman to apply the passenger car brakes. He then jumped to the ground to avoid death. His fireman, however, died in the wreck.

After several days of fact-finding and deliberations, the jury released its report on August 14:

> *The said collision was the immediate result of the culpable carelessness, inexperience, and want of judgment of Frederick W. Putnam, conductor of the down train, in leaving the station at Valley Falls when he had but four minutes, by his time, to reach Boston Switch—which, we say, was a disregard of the railroad company's orders and instructions, and in not providing himself with a suitable and correct watch—his time proving to be two minutes behind the true time which he set by the Company's clock in Providence the night before the collision took place. We also blame the Managers of the road for appointing so young and inexperienced a man such as Mr. Putnam to be the conductor of the Whitinsville train, one of the most difficult to manage. We also blame the Managers for not providing Conductors with a suitable and correct watch to run their trains by.*
>
> *We also say the up train from Providence, in which the President and Superintendent of the Railroad Company were riding with an experienced Conductor, should have started from Boston Switch the very second the signal was given; by so doing it might have reached a point on the road where it would have been in sight from the Valley Falls Station and the great calamity would have probably been avoided, which, we say, is attributable to the Conductor of the Providence up train who permitted Freeman, its engineer, and the brakeman, to be absent from their posts when the signal to start was given.[28]*

The very first image of a train wreck in America: the head-on collision of two trains at Valley Falls, Rhode Island, on the Providence and Worcester Railroad. The cause? Human error.

The coroner subsequently had conductor Putnam arrested for manslaughter, and the case went to the Rhode Island Supreme Court the following month. Putnam, who usually received thirty dollars a month from the company for his services, was of course terminated, as was engineer Gates, along with the "master of transportation" at Uxbridge.

Two sidebars: the Valley Falls event was the first railroad wreck in America to be photographed—a daguerreotype composed by one L. Wright. In their own effort to determine who was responsible for the blunder, the railroad commissioners of Rhode Island stated that they did not find any one person guilty of recklessness or carelessness at Valley Falls, that the variations in Putnam's watch combined with the close running of trains were the attributed causes and that only the company's managers needed censure.[29]

Freight trains and an occasional passenger train still transit the busy Providence and Worcester, which today is owned by the Genesee and

Wyoming Railroad. The P&W's footprint, too, has expanded through the years, and Valley Falls remains an important service point. But the disaster that happened there in 1853, some 170 years ago, is—for most—nothing more than a distant memory.

CHAPTER 3

MASSACHUSETTS (PART I)

REVERE, AUGUST 26, 1871

Many—but not all—railroad disasters that have happened in New England are remembered to this day. One that seems to be forever etched in the public's memory was the tragic rear-end collision that occurred in Revere in the nineteenth century. Twenty-nine people perished in the horrid event, and nearly sixty were injured. That the disaster aroused the wrath of individuals and publications across America is an understatement.

The catastrophe took place on the Eastern Railroad, which operated a main line route between Boston and Portland, Maine, via Everett, Revere, Lynn, Portsmouth and Kennebunk. It also possessed numerous branch lines. Known for accidents, buying politicians and graft, the firm nevertheless did a remarkable business. "During the winter months leading up to the Revere disaster, as many as 75,000 passengers were conveyed by the railroad weekly. In the summertime, because of extra excursions and pleasure travel, nearly 110,000 persons were transported."[30] However, the availability of rolling stock was often taxed to the limit during those summer months, with trains often departing late from Boston with little regard for safety. Riding the bottleneck of impatient travelers from the "Hub of the Universe" was an unspoken priority.

In the week ending Saturday, August 26, 1871, the demands placed on the Eastern were enormous. "The number of passengers seeking transit over the road weekly had accordingly risen to over 142,000; while the regular number of 152 freight and passenger trains was increased to 191. Much confusion in the operation of the road necessarily resulted from this condition of affairs, and, during the day of the [Revere] accident, trains arrived and left the station in Boston in very considerable disregard of their regular times."[31] That Jeremiah Prescott, the Eastern's conservative superintendent, forbade the use of the telegraph to dispatch trains added to the chaos. Before the great Revere disaster, "his method of dispatching trains was such that on at least one occasion an Eastern freight train waited all night at Salem for an extra passenger train, which in turn spent the night at Ipswich, waiting for the freight."[32]

As August ended, passenger traffic out of Boston was immense, owing, in part, to the region's sweltering dog days.

> *People lay under the elms on the Common, sticky and motionless. In many quarters of the South End, kids turned on fire hydrants while adults tried to find relief on fire escapes. No cooling breezes found their way even through the handsome open windows on Beacon Hill. The Bostonians who could afford it were trying to get out of town to one of the brisk and salty places along the North Shore or in Maine.*[33]

The railroad's main line was supplemented with a loop (or secondary) track between Everett and Lynn—called the Saugus Branch—which meandered inland. Ball signals, positioned on masts and operated by rope pulleys, controlled train movements between the two junction points. They were operated by signalmen, who also manipulated nearby track switches. Unfortunately, no side track existed at Everett Junction for trains to meet or wait. At Revere station, another ball signal and set of switches guarded the branch that led down to East Boston.

On the evening of August 26, four trains were scheduled to depart Boston, in succession, between 6:30 and 8:00 p.m.—a Saugus Branch train at 6:30, a second Saugus Branch train at 7:00, the Beverly accommodation at 7:15 and the fast Portland Express at 8:00 p.m. All would leave late and out of order. First to depart was the first Saugus Branch train at 7:00, followed by the Beverly accommodation at 7:40 and the second Saugus Branch train at 7:53, while the Portland Express got underway about five minutes past eight o'clock. As noted, the two Saugus Branch trains were switched at Everett, while the Beverly accommodation and the Portland Express remained on the main track. Initially, the latter two trains had about forty-five minutes of separation time between them, but because the Beverly train had been delayed, this was reduced to about twenty-five minutes. "This was a simple case of a slow accommodation train being sent out to run 18 miles in front of a fast express train."[34]

As luck would have it, another operational problem arose that evening. A southbound train coming down the Saugus Branch from Lynn had yet to arrive at Everett Junction, which prevented the two Saugus Branch trains from leaving until it arrived and departed. Wedged between the two Branch trains stood the Beverly accommodation. And before long, the Portland Express eased to a stop behind the trio. Had the telegraph been in use, the congestion could have been easily averted.

The southbound train finally arrived and cleared Everett Junction, whereupon the substitute and inexperienced signalman managed to shuffle and seesaw the four standing trains. Once the first Saugus Branch train got underway, the next to depart was the Beverly accommodation. Then, the second branch train left, followed by the fast-moving Express. (The engineer of the Express incorrectly thought the Beverly accommodation had long since departed Everett.) In short order, about five minutes would separate the Express from the accommodation train.

As the two trains approached the Revere station, they were so close to each other as to be on the same piece of straight track at the same time, and the headlight on the locomotive of the Portland Express was distinctly seen by a passenger standing at the rear end of the Beverly train. The night was not a clear one. The interval between the two trains was probably less than a mile when the Beverly accommodation reached Revere.[35]

After making its station stop at Revere, the Beverly train began to leave. But its conductor, seeing the oncoming headlight, at once sprang onto the track, waving his lantern as a signal of danger. The engineer of the Express had already signaled danger and reversed his engine, while the car brakes were being rapidly set by the brakemen. The engineer and fireman then jumped to the ground to avoid death. Because the brakes had been applied and the engine's driving wheels had been reversed, the speed of the Express was reduced to about ten miles per hour.

Nevertheless, the Express train's locomotive violently smashed into the rear coach of the Beverly train with such force as to bury itself into nearly its entire length.

The smokestack of the locomotive was swept away…and the entire boiler rested inside and upon the rear truck of the passenger car, while its boiler valves were so broken as to admit the free escape of scalding steam. There were about 65–70 passengers in the car, seated and standing—men, women, and children. As the colliding locomotive moved through the coach it crushed furniture, fixtures, and human beings into a maze.[36]

The lighted kerosene lamps in all the coaches at once fell to the floor and started the cars ablaze, helped by the live coals from the engine's firebox. A scene of indescribable horror unfolded in that last car, from passengers being scalded to death by live steam to many being burned alive.

The collision at Revere resulted from a combination of causes and defects of management—all preventable—but some of them peculiar to the Eastern Railroad. Among the causes that the railroad commissioners of Massachusetts cited in their exhaustive investigation report (found in their 1873 annual report; see Notes) was a laxity of discipline in the movement of trains and obeying rules; the nonuse of the telegraph in dispatching trains;

The fiery rear-end collision at Revere aroused enormous criticism of train travel. A famous orator of the day, the fiery abolitionist Wendell Phillips, hailed the wreck as "deliberate murder."

the general confusion in and around the station at Boston; the lack of a side track at Everett Junction; and excessive business that imperiled safety.

Reactions by the public and publications were swift and devastating. Among those vehemently criticizing the Eastern's deplorable ways (and that of railroads in general) was Wendell Phillips, the great Boston abolitionist, reformer and orator. After the disaster, mass meetings of protest were staged in various Massachusetts cities, and Phillips was often the fiery speaker. He would insist over and over that the Revere disaster was "deliberate murder."[37]

The Eastern eventually paid out about a half million dollars to settle claims, but its directors could never arrest the negative publicity. In 1884, the stigmatized firm was leased to the Boston and Maine Railroad, which acquired the Eastern in 1890.

Wollaston, October 8, 1878

The Old Colony Railroad was—in the latter nineteenth century—a force to be reckoned with in southeastern Massachusetts and Rhode Island. Its trains fanned out from Boston to such destinations as Plymouth, Fall River, New Bedford, Newport, Providence, Fitchburg, Lowell and Cape Cod. It also controlled steamboat and ferry lines, among them the famed Fall River Line, whose vessels were noted for their luxurious accommodations and conveniences. By 1893, when it was acquired by the New York, New Haven and Hartford Railroad Company, the Old Colony possessed nearly 620 miles of rail lines. Acquisitions and mergers had largely made this possible, the successful enterprise having first opened between Boston and Plymouth back in 1845.

Railway wrecks and accidents were not foreign to the Old Colony, and the 1878 disaster in the Wollaston neighborhood of Quincy would result from— of all things—a misaligned track switch. Nineteen persons were killed in the freak disaster, and some 170 were injured. The conductor who misplaced the switch, which derailed an excursion passenger train, was convicted of manslaughter, although his conviction was later overturned.

On October 8, a spectacular rowing event drew a huge crowd to Silver Lake in the town of Plympton. To transport spectators, the Old Colony ran a special excursion train from and to Boston, consisting of two locomotives, a baggage car, an "English-style" compartment car and nineteen ordinary passenger coaches. After the big event, the enthralled passengers left Silver Lake station at 6:00 p.m. and reached Wollaston, in darkness, at 7:19 p.m. A bulletin or circular had been distributed earlier among train employees that gave the excursion train a general right of way over the railroad, specifically on its inbound or inward track to Boston after 4:00 p.m. without a set time schedule. In fact, when the disaster occurred, the train was already some two hours late.

That same evening, a southbound freight train departed Boston for Newport at 6:30 p.m. It left on the railroad's outbound or outward track and consisted of an engine and tender and fifteen freight cars. That it departed Boston short-handed—it did not have a front-end brakeman—was a grave and direct violation of company rules that gave the railroad company "an unwarranted assumption of risk." (The train's conductor, Charles Hartwell, had excused the brakeman from working that day because he was ill.) Thus, the crew that evening was composed of the engineer, a fireman, a rear brakeman and Hartwell.

Like other train employees, Hartwell had received and read the circular about the Silver Lake excursion special, "but as he occupied only the outbound track, while the special was on the inbound, the notice contained no reference to his train. He was left to the guidance of the general rules, which were specific and well understood."[38] Among those rules was this directive: that if Hartwell needed to cross over the inbound track to perhaps reach a siding or to temporarily occupy any portion of it while switching, he or his train employees had to safeguard both the outbound and inbound tracks using flags or lanterns. From the moment he left Boston, Hartwell was under the distinct belief that the Silver Lake special had already arrived in Boston.

As part of his work that night, Hartwell had to pick up five empty flat cars on the Wollaston Iron Foundry siding, located slightly north of town. He arrived there before seven o'clock, short-handed as noted, and fully possessed with the idea that the special had already reached Boston.

> *The five flat cars were on the siding together with a box car loaded with sand. To get to the flat cars, it was necessary to haul the box-car also off the siding onto the outbound track and then, after getting the flats out of the way, to shove the box-car back into the siding. To accomplish this to-and-fro switching meant crossing the inbound track and occupying it for some considerable time.*[39]

The rear brakeman proceeded to throw the necessary switches, and the engine was uncoupled from the train.

> *This done, the engineer backed his locomotive over the connecting switch and the crossover onto the inbound track, and thence onto the siding where the freight cars stood. These were then coupled on, and the whole started forward to rejoin the freight train. The solitary brakeman was upon the box-car next to the locomotive while Hartwell was on the rear flat, or sixth car. There was no flagman and both main tracks were broken—the outbound being occupied by the freight train and the inbound track being left connected with the siding as the box-car was to be immediately returned to it.*[40]

It should be noted that the switches were of the Tyler patent, which had lanterns that displayed red when opened.

While moving to the outbound track, engineer Westgate of Hartwell's train caught sight of something quite unexpected: the headlight of the lead locomotive of the Silver Lake special about a half mile away. He at once "put on steam" and called to his fireman to wave a red lantern. Unfortunately, the glare of the approaching headlight was so strong as to obscure the lantern and the red switch signals. However, the engineer managed to get all the cars attached to the engine out of the way of the approaching train. No collision took place, but the siding switch was set wrong. The special should, therefore, have entered the siding, where it would have stopped.

The engineer of the special's lead locomotive saw the headlight of the freight engine as it passed to the outbound track and supposed that it belonged to some outbound train in its proper place. He paid no further attention to it, but when about three hundred feet from the freight engine, he saw the red lantern while at the same time his fireman caught sight of the red switch signal. "As his was the leading locomotive, he did not have control of the train-brake."[41] He at once signaled danger with the locomotive whistle and reversed his engine. The engineer of the second locomotive immediately set the Westinghouse brake, thus checking the train, which was then running at the speed of twenty miles an hour. He, too, reversed his engine.

Hartwell himself caught sight of the oncoming special about the same time as his engineer, whence he jumped off the last flat car and ran to one of the switches. Which one he ran to was conflicting in his testimony. "The most plausible theory," according to the Massachusetts railroad commissioner's investigation report, "is that he attempted to throw over the siding switch to keep the coming train on the inbound track. He did not, however, have enough time to fully do so."[42]

Hartwell not being fully successful, the special's two locomotives, its baggage car and six passenger cars subsequently derailed at the unclosed siding

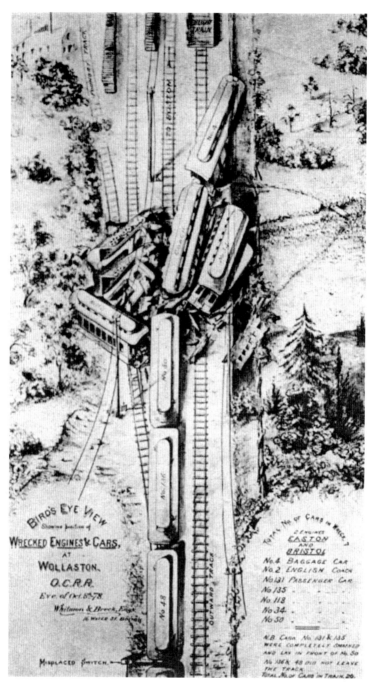

An interesting bird's-eye view of the deadly wreck at Wollaston on the Old Colony Railroad. A confused conductor had not fully engaged a siding switch, which derailed a passenger train.

switch and left the track. Its two engines then swung left and toppled over, while many of the cars were thrown to one side or the other. Some telescoped, others were crushed; the two cars behind the English coach were reduced to mere fragments. The cylinder of the second engine even tore loose and ripped open one entire side of the English car, killing or maiming nearly all inside. All four men in charge of the two locomotives, though flung violently into the trees and ditch beside the railroad, were neither seriously injured nor stunned and managed to prevent fire from spreading to the train's cars.[43]

Both the conductor and engineer of the freight train were found guilty of gross and criminal negligence. Hartwell was cited for taking his train out short-handed; leaving his train on the outbound track without protecting its rear; occupying the inbound track without protecting it while so doing; and causing switches to be changed and leaving them changed without protection. Engineer Westgate was found guilty of occupying the inbound track without protection. The railroad commissioners ordered the arrest of Hartwell, who was held on $10,000 bail. On February 27, 1880, however, his conviction was overturned on a technicality by the Massachusetts Supreme Judicial Court. The misplaced or misaligned switch at Wollaston garnered national attention and became something of a new cause of railroad wrecks.

Roslindale, March 14, 1887

One of the first railroads to open in the Bay State was the Boston and Providence, which began service between its namesake cities in 1835. Its landmark engineering achievement—the famed viaduct in Canton—still stands and is used daily by Amtrak trains and other carriers. Desirous of new traffic, the company wasted little time in building a branch from its main line to the burgeoning community of Dedham, and it was on the Dedham Branch that the infamous Bussey Bridge disaster occurred. The bridge stood over South Street in Roslindale, and among the views commuters enjoyed on the branch were those of the old Bussey farm.

The commuter train involved in this 1887 disaster left Dedham station for Boston at seven o'clock in the morning. Aside from an engine and tender, the train was composed of nine cars, with the last one being a combination baggage and smoking car. There were approximately 275 to 300 people on the train; 23 would die in the bridge calamity, and over 100 would be seriously injured. Many of the train's passengers were residents of Roslindale.

The Bussey Bridge was originally built of wood to the famous Howe design so popular on American railroads. It was later "tinned" to protect it from fire and thus acquired the nickname of the "Tin Bridge." In 1870, the western wooden truss was replaced with a rectangular one of iron, built by the National Bridge Company. Six years later, the eastern wooden truss was replaced with one of iron fabricated by the Metropolitan Bridge Company. In the process, the truss built by National was moved to the east side of the bridge, while the Metropolitan one was erected on the west side. Unbeknownst to anyone, there existed no Metropolitan company per se; it was created strictly in the mind of Edmund H. Hewins, a civil engineer and its supposed proprietor. Nevertheless, his firm got the contract. It was eventually revealed, however, that faulty construction methods and substandard materials were used by Hewins, and the disaster that resulted centered not only on those issues but also on gross negligence by the railroad company for not carefully investigating the builder, or his bogus firm, and for not—over the years—intelligently and thoroughly inspecting the structure.[44]

Engineer White—a railway veteran of thirty-one years—testified that when the commuter train came upon the Bussey Bridge that fateful morning, everything seemed normal at first; there was no settling or swinging. But when he came to the Boston end of the bridge, the front of his engine produced a jar, the driving wheels somewhat reared and he felt a shock. He looked back and saw that the first car had derailed and broken away because its coupling had failed. White reversed his engine, looked back again and now saw the second car had derailed; both were swinging to the right side of the bridge. A cloud of smoke then arose, a definite indication that cars had gone through the bridge.

The engineer brought his engine to a quick stop, again reversed direction and dashed to Forest Hills. He blew the whistle nonstop, and as people came out of their homes, he pointed back to the bridge. Another train was ready to depart Forest Hills for Dedham. White told its engineer and conductor of the bridge failure, and off they went to aid those in distress. White then went inside the Forest Hills station and told the agent to summon doctors and ambulances. The railroad's superintendent in Roxbury was also notified, and another rescue train was dispatched. The helpful and quick-thinking engineer then returned to the wreck site.[45]

The cause of the disaster started on the north half of the bridge, specifically by the breaking of the hangers on the joint block at the north end of the truss built by Hewins. (The hangers, over many years, had been overstressed.) Bridge experts engaged for the investigations confirmed this,

The Bussey Bridge over South Street in Roslindale, prior to its collapse. The bridge was regarded as peculiar in design and appearance, and it was later discovered that integral modifications had been carried out by a bogus company.

which included Professor George Vose of the Massachusetts Institute of Technology. "I think that bridge, in its general plan and in its details, was a standing invitation to be knocked to pieces. The thing was waiting to tumble down."[46] Unfortunately, the hangers themselves were concealed and could not be observed during inspections by railroad authorities or the railroad commissioners of Massachusetts. The latter's exhaustive investigation report, with all the testimony, would be ordered published by the legislature. The lengthy publication (some 420 pages) is now available online or can be purchased.[47]

According to the commission's investigation, "The strain which broke the hangers was probably given when the engine's driving wheels passed over them, and there was a slight depression of the bridge when the engine left it. This depression increased when the first car left the bridge."[48] The other cars followed and contributed to the stress, whereupon the bridge collapsed. The cars ended up in a deadly mass on the embankments and South Street. Most of the people who were killed were in the fourth, fifth, sixth and ninth cars.

The so-called hangers held up the floor beams of the bridge. When the beams fell, the floor system then fell. It never occurred to those who built

When the Bussey Bridge collapsed, the cars of a Dedham commuter train piled up in South Street and nearby embankments. Many passengers were instantly killed or seriously injured.

or inspected the bridge that the strength and condition of the hangers was so vital. The railroad company would admit in the investigation that it had no scale drawings or exact specifications of the hangers or of Hewins's work in general. Incidental to the disaster, but not the fault of Hewins, was the fact that crossties under the rails on the bridge were not correctly spaced apart, even after the railroad company had been warned of this violation.

The railroad commissioners made the following conclusions after their lengthy investigation: the railroad company did not properly investigate the credentials or the contract of Hewins; those who made the contract for the railroad did not have sufficient knowledge of iron bridge building; the

An artist's sketch of the Bussey Bridge carnage on the Dedham Branch of the Boston and Providence Railroad. New regulations governing bridge inspections and construction were immediately enacted in Massachusetts.

design and specifications of Hewins's work should not have been accepted; the bridge work of Hewins proceeded without superintendence by the railroad; and the stress tests of the bridge were not conducted by anyone connected with the railroad who was qualified to judge their value.[49]

Today, a stone arch railroad bridge spans South Street in Roslindale, and Needham Line trains of the Massachusetts Bay Transit Authority pass over it every day. On its north wall is a plaque commemorating the terrible disaster that happened here nearly 140 years ago.

BRADFORD, JANUARY 10, 1888

Sometimes called the Haverhill Bridge wreck, this railway disaster actually took place across the Merrimack River in nearby Bradford. No better synopsis of the catastrophe appeared than in *Harper's Weekly* illustrated newspaper:

The never-ending catalog of railway accidents contains not a single one stranger than that at Bradford. A "butcher's bill" [naval slang for the dead and wounded after a battle] *of twelve dead and over thirty injured is unhappily not very remarkable. The marvel lies in the almost unprecedented and most shocking manner in which these unfortunate people were killed and maimed.*

The little Bradford station is perhaps 500 feet from the Merrimac River, which the Boston and Maine Railroad, curving to the left, crosses by a bridge having a 500-foot span and is 80 feet above the water. Between the station and the bridge is a switch curving to the right and heading to the Georgetown branch railway. In the angle of the Y formed where the railways come together is, or was, a tank holding 100,000 gallons of water.

The unfortunate train was an express, which was to pass Bradford without stopping. The track and switch signals were all right, and so the engineer dashed along at a speed estimated by himself at fifteen miles an hour, but by experienced passengers at from thirty to forty miles. The locomotive, tender, and three cars passed over the branch switch safely, but the smoking car was derailed there. A large piece was afterward found to be broken from the flange of a wheel, and that, the railway authorities say, is the cause of what followed.

The smoking car, the fourth car on the train, bumped over the ties and the stringers of the bridge past the abutment on the river's brink. It careened fearfully to the right and then to the left, coming to rest on its side, with thirty or forty people flung pell-mell into the roof. The passenger car next to the smoker left the track, as fate would have it, near the water tank, and dashing beneath it, knocked out its supports. No serious harm had yet been done, but gravity completed the disaster. The large structure of boiler-iron, weighing with its contents not less than a million pounds, fell and ground almost to a powder the car, the unfortunate people within it, along with a little group of railway employees who an instant before had been merrily chatting and eating their mid-day meal.

Amazingly, the car next behind the crushed one took to the tracks of the Georgetown railway and ran without serious injury into a train standing there! The rear car of the express ran into the debris of the water tank, but also without much harm. All the survivors say the awful flood of tank water suggested to them they were drowning in the river. Perhaps the most pitiful incident of all was the taking from the train of a father, mother, and child, all crushed to a jelly.[50]

Naturally, the railroad commissioners of Massachusetts conducted a formal investigation of the Bradford disaster and attached a very thorough account to their 1888 annual report to the legislature. A few ancillary facts: the train in question was the one o'clock express from Boston, and among the other cars were a baggage car and a milk car; a four-degree curve existed just before the Boston and Maine track turned toward the Merrimac River; and the speed restriction on the bridge was not to exceed fifteen miles per hour, which engineer Warren French said, in testimony, that he was about to obey.

"That portion of the track where the accident happened," said the commissioners, "combines many elements of danger. There is a curve with a long down grade tangent on one end and a bridge on the other. On the outside of this curve, near the middle, is a switch leading to a branch track.

In foreground: the train involved in the Bradford wreck has just been re-railed. Note the damaged smoking car. The branch to the extreme right, after the station, went to Georgetown. The city of Haverhill is in the distance.

A branch track leading from the main track is always an element of danger, and the most dangerous place for such a branch to start from is from the outside of a curve."[51]

Perhaps the most damning statement of the commissioners was this:

> *An inquiry in regard to the method of inspecting wheels showed that the inspection to which the wheels on this train were subjected the day of the accident was a lamentable mockery. Charles Farnum, for twenty years a car inspector and having charge of the Prison Point car house, testified that he inspected the wheels of this train on the morning of the accident; that the wheels on the smoking-car were chilled iron and not much worn; that he examined the wheels inside and outside of the car house; and did not rap them but trusted his eyesight; and that rapping them merely produced a good impression upon the public.*[52]

The commissioners thus began an inquiry into the merits of steel-tired wheels versus those of chilled iron.

From their investigation, the commissioners made the following recommendations: such accidents like Bradford must be immediately reported to the commission, not delayed; photographs of such accidents needed to be taken before anything was disturbed; a water tank must always be placed on the inside, not outside, of a curve; the ties on such a bridge should be separated, if needed, with spring blocks; the switch to the Georgetown branch should be moved back and installed on tangent track; and the training of car inspectors needed improving.[53]

Trains still very much come and go through Bradford, and those of the MBTA often stop at its modern station. The bridge over the Merrimack has been refurbished, but the branch to Georgetown is ancient history. Hopefully, future generations will not forget what happened in Bradford that fateful day in 1888.

CHAPTER 4

MASSACHUSETTS (PART II)

Quincy, August 19, 1890

In the previous chapter, we encountered the Wollaston wreck on the Old Colony Railroad caused by a misaligned track switch. The disaster described here would also occur on the Old Colony, this time by another peril: a piece of equipment carelessly left on a track for a train to strike and derail. In this event, twenty-four lives were lost and some thirty persons were seriously injured.

The train that struck the rail "jack" (not dissimilar to an automobile jack) was the Colony's popular Vineyard, Nantucket and Hyannis Express. The train had left Woods Hole at 10:45 a.m. and was due in Boston at 1:10 p.m. The derailment and subsequent wreck took place shortly after the train passed the Quincy station, at a point just north of the Dimmock Street bridge. Twelve persons were killed instantly or died before they could be taken from the wreck; others perished afterward from injuries. With the exception of locomotive fireman James Ryan, all the fatalities occurred in the fourth car.[54]

The train comprised an engine and tender, a baggage car, a Pullman, a smoking car, three passenger cars, a combination car, a fourth passenger car and an additional combination car. The first six cars originated at Woods Hole, and the last three came from the company's Cape division and were added at Buzzards Bay. About 390 persons were aboard the train. Charles Babcock was the train's engineer.

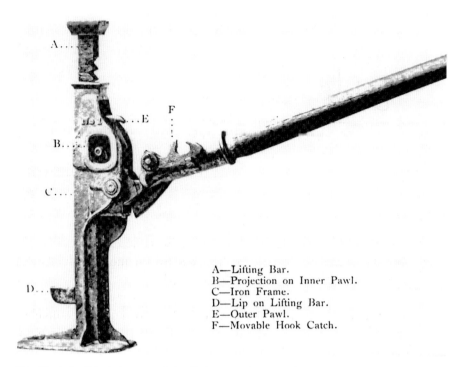

A—Lifting Bar.
B—Projection on Inner Pawl.
C—Iron Frame.
D—Lip on Lifting Bar.
E—Outer Pawl.
F—Movable Hook Catch.

The kind of rail jack that caused the Quincy wreck on the Old Colony Railroad. A track worker could lug the cumbersome item about, but two made it easier. A jack left on the track was hit by a train, which then derailed.

It was at the end of a curve that the derailment and resulting wreck took place. The Old Colony ran its trains left-handed—that is, the inbound or inward track was on the left and the outbound or outward was on the right side. The train was due to pass the Quincy station at 12:56 p.m. but was running about seven minutes late. Babcock's speed was about twenty-five miles per hour.

About this time, an outbound train transporting thirty cars of gravel went past Babcock on the opposite track. Its engineer made a motion to him that he should whistle for people on the track ahead, as the gravel train engineer thought that the noise of his train would prevent the people from hearing the approach of the passenger train. "Immediately, the engineer of the Express saw section men at work on the track, about 350-feet from him, and he gave short, sharp whistles to warn them of his approach."[55]

There were about eight to ten workers laboring on the track, and upon hearing the warning whistles, they quickly left their work. But by the time they all had retreated, Babcock was about 100 to 150 feet from where they had been working. He then observed something frightful: a worker had left a jack on the inside of the westerly rail, a short distance north of the Dimmock Street overhead bridge. Babcock immediately put the train brake into the emergency position. From that moment on, he had "no clear idea of what happened from that time until he found himself on top of the boiler of the engine after the accident."[56]

While Babcock successfully applied the train brake, he did not engage the reverse lever (to reverse the engine's driving wheels to also slow the train), nor did he engage the engine's dedicated brake handle, primarily because—upon seeing the jack—he had only about four seconds to react. The engine was not immediately derailed until it reached a point thirty feet from the jack. Then, it jumped the track to the west toward a ditch and not toward the outbound track. After hitting the jack, the engine continued on about 280 feet, toppled over and stopped with its front end driven into an embankment and its rear end projecting over the inbound track.

The engine's tender, which carried coal and water, ended up on the inbound track about two hundred feet beyond the locomotive, completely turned around. Along its length was the baggage car, lying on its side on the outbound track minus its wheels. (The baggage master and conductor Steadman, who were within, escaped without injury.) Behind the baggage car, also on the outbound track, was the Pullman car Puritan, which stood in line with the track, minus its wheel trucks. The fixed chairs, mirrors and windows therein were "uninjured." The smoker car was jammed against the rear platform of the Pullman, minus wheels, and rested diagonally between the two tracks. Some of its occupants were seriously injured.

The train's fourth car, in reality the first coach, was lying across the inbound track, tipped over to its left side, which was torn out by the collision with the rear end of the engine. The rear driving wheel of the engine projected into this car to about its middle. "It was a total wreck, being fearfully twisted and torn." The next passenger coach was also on the inbound track, "largely uninjured." The train's other four cars remained on the rails and were in a condition to be at once removed.[57]

The position of the cars indicates that, when the engine stopped, the thrust of the nine cars behind turned the tender around on its connection with the engine; and, in turning, the tender operated as a wedge to force the baggage car off the inbound track onto the outbound track. The link and pin connection between the baggage car and tender held, while the shackle and chain connection between the engine and tender broke.[58]

The derailment at Quincy spun the engine of the derailed train around, and it landed on a nearby track, as did several cars.

Within the fourth car (the first passenger coach) were seventy passengers, the largest number of any car. As noted, the locomotive crashed into it, and many persons were crushed and pinned down by the framework of the engine and debris. Steam and hot water from broken pipes sprayed about and fatally scalded many passengers. From the debris behind the driving wheels of the engine, many corpses were later removed, including that of locomotive fireman Ryan, who, because of his position, could not be extracted until some three hours after the wreck.

Members of the Massachusetts railroad commission along with Old Colony general manager Kendrick were at the scene shortly after the accident took place. Kendrick informed the commissioners that the wreck had been caused by a rail jack being left on the track. The section gang who used it had just returned from their midday meal. The worker in charge of the jack, Michael Hartney, was identified and insisted he had no way of knowing when trains were due and that he relied on his section foreman, Joseph Welch, for such information and protection. Hartney had received no order from his foreman to remove the jack and knew not when the express was coming, but when he heard the warning whistles,

A better view of the carnage at Quincy. The jack left on the track was later discovered in a nearby ditch. The men sporting straw boaters could possibly be railway officials or state railroad commissioners.

he jumped for his life. Nine seconds would pass between the whistles and his jump. The jack, manufactured by Barrett, was found in a ditch at the side of the track. The immediate responsibility for the Quincy disaster fell on Joseph Welch, the section master, whose most inexcusable neglect was his failure to keep a lookout posted for oncoming trains. He was arrested on manslaughter charges. The railroad commissioners, in their investigation report, also found fault with the brakes and braking action of the train.

CHESTER, AUGUST 31, 1893

Within the picturesque Berkshire foothills of western Massachusetts lies the rural village of Chester. The famed Western Railroad arrived here in 1841, and in 1867, the company merged with the Boston and Worcester to form the Boston and Albany Railroad. It was the latter firm that would experience the painful tragedy at Chester.

The cause of the disaster was not complicated: bridge workers, making improvements to Willcutt's Bridge over the west branch of the Westfield River in Chester, had gone to lunch and left key elements of the structure unattached and unsafe for railway traffic. A crack passenger train crossed it at 12:30 p.m., and the bridge collapsed. Fourteen people died; twice that number were seriously injured.

Train No. 16—the Chicago Express—consisted of a ten-wheel locomotive (No. 12, one of the railroad's largest and heaviest passenger train engines) and seven cars arranged as follows: a combination baggage and buffet car, two Wagner sleeping cars, a dining car, two ordinary coaches and a smoking car. The combination car and the two sleepers came through from Chicago, the diner was attached at Utica and the two coaches and smoker were added at Albany. Upon departing that capital, 42 persons occupied the combination car and Wagner sleepers, and 93 persons were in the three rear coaches—135 in all. Ultimately, 9 passengers would die in the Chester wreck along with 5 train employees.[59]

In the words of the railroad commissioners of Massachusetts, the wreck was particularly sad because it happened on a road having high standards of construction and equipment. In fact, it was "making liberal and increasing expenditures for the safety and comfort of travelers on its line. The Boston & Albany has been surpassed in these respects by no other railroad corporation in New England, and perhaps by none in this country."[60]

The commission, spearheaded years before by member Charles Francis Adams Jr. and highly regarded in America, had a twofold charge in performing its investigation: to find out "at whose door the responsibility for the catastrophe lies in order that the delinquent may be held to answer at the bar of public opinion if not of the courts, and to discover the safeguards, if any, whose omissions caused or permitted the disaster, and whose adoption may avert the recurrence of similar casualties in the future."[61] The quality of their investigation reports were exceptional, and the one written about Chester was no exception. It followed standards first created by Adams, who resided in Quincy, whose grandfather and great-grandfather were presidents of the United States. Adams Jr. would later become a president of the Union Pacific Railroad.

Commission members visited the Chester wreck on the day it occurred and on subsequent days. Assisting them was George Swain, professor of civil engineering at the Massachusetts Institute of Technology. A bridge expert, Swain arrived a day after the wreck from western travels. Per his request, nothing at the wreck site had been disturbed. Public hearings, held by the commission, would occupy three days, and the testimony of some thirty witnesses was received—twelve of whom were connected with the railroad and sixteen of whom were from the R.F. Hawkins Iron Works in Springfield and were performing work on the bridge at the time of the accident.

The bridge was built in 1874 by Niagara Bridge of Buffalo on plans by Edward Philbrick, "an engineer of distinction in his day." It was a "double-track through bridge" of iron having two spans, each about 104 feet in length, with two trusses for each span. Through the years, it had required only ordinary attention and repairs. It was inspected monthly and rendered satisfactory deflection results just a few weeks prior to the wreck. There were no signs of structural weakness or deterioration, and it had not received or required alteration or strengthening.

In Professor Swain's earlier report of 1891, he noted to the commission that the "floor" of the bridge at Chester was too light for Consolidation-type engines, and it should be strengthened before such were allowed to pass over it. In 1893, railroad president George Bliss—foreseeing Consolidation and ten-wheel passenger locomotives coming into use between Pittsfield and Springfield—ordered the floor of the Chester bridge strengthened. He also decided to have the bridge's trusses strengthened. The job was wholly "a work of strengthening and consisted chiefly of more iron plates and shapes to those already forming a part of the structure of the bridge."[62]

The contract for the above work was drawn up with the aforementioned Hawkins company. One of the firm's employees, J. Dana Reed, acted as "outside superintendent" of the various bridge projects that were to occur between Pittsfield and Springfield. But he did not supervise the daily work. That was left to a foreman and gang of workers who were employed at each site. Thirteen men worked the Chester contract. Its foreman was Daniel Belville, thirty-six years old, an employee of Hawkins for fifteen years. Among his duties, in addition to supervising, was to signal trains in case of an emergency. The railroad's master carpenter and bridge builder, as well as its bridge inspector for the division, understood "rightly or wrongly" that their functions were suspended while the work was being carried out by Hawkins and "that they had no business in any way to meddle with it."[63] Thus, the railroad company had no direct supervision of the work or really knew the condition of the bridge during such.

According to the commission's report of the wreck, the work done did not demand any high degree of mechanical knowledge or skill. A gang of riveters was needed along with common laborers and helpers. The work basically entailed putting new cover-plates on the posts or chords of each truss to strengthen them; the old rivets had been taken out before new ones were installed. Because the removal process of the rivets temporarily weakened the trusses, it was imperative to install the new rivets as quickly as possible, otherwise the rivet holes had to be temporarily fitted with bolts or drift pins. The work was timed to the running of trains.

On the day of the accident, a few workmen were finishing odd jobs about the bridge. The rest of the gang was working on the top chord of the southerly truss of the western span, next to the eastbound track. The riveters had finished installing new rivets on the first panel of the chord, at the extreme west end of the bridge, while other workmen had to cut off or back out the old rivets on the panels toward the middle of the chord.

Around eleven o'clock that morning, an engine and two flat cars, carrying a load of iron for the bridge, came down from Chester station—a little more than a mile west—and proceeded to cross the bridge. Belville, the foreman, walked in back of the train and called out to the workers to follow him and help unload the iron on the other side of the bridge. The workers obeyed but left the truss chord in a dangerous state. Most everyone was busy unloading the iron until noon, when the foreman announced it was time for lunch. The workers scattered. Belville then walked back across the bridge, making sure there was no debris left on the two tracks, whence he proceeded to his boardinghouse for lunch. A local passenger train passed over the bridge at about 12:20 p.m. without incident.

As noted, the cover plates on the southwesterly corner, both old and new, of the truss chord remained unfastened for some twenty-five feet while the workers ate lunch. No new rivets or bolts or drift pins had been temporarily installed. Further, the lateral braces were wholly disconnected from the top chord of both trusses—the number of empty rivet holes numbering not fewer than one hundred. The bridge, according to the commission's report, had been "radically and fatally weakened."

The heavily laden Chicago Express charged across the structure at maybe thirty miles per hour, having passed Chester station six minutes late. No train orders or bulletins had been issued to slow down trains for the construction work. Once on the bridge, it gave way, and the regrettable carnage and loss of life followed, whereupon the rescue of passengers and train personnel began.[64] It was, according to all accounts, a horrible scene.

The immediate party responsible for the disaster at Chester was foreman Belville for leaving the bridge in an unsafe condition while he and his workers went to lunch. Neither the train crew nor the speed of the train played a direct or contributing role to the collapse. The railroad, in turn,

A close-up of cars belonging to the Chicago Express at the bridge collapse in Chester on the Boston and Albany Railroad. The cause was carelessness and human error.

was censured for not having on duty a competent supervisor to monitor the work as it progressed.

Needless to say, President Bliss and his senior executives were devastated by the Chester wreck, primarily because—up until that point—the Boston and Albany had such an enviable safety record and was admired as a well-built and efficiently operated railroad. A dark shadow, indeed, now hung over the corporation.

LINCOLN, NOVEMBER 26, 1905

The ghastly wreck at Lincoln—also known as the Baker Bridge Disaster—was a classic rear-end collision that killed sixteen persons and injured twenty-five. Like all other tragedies detailed in this book, the one at Lincoln had its unique elements. The wreck took place on the Boston and Maine Railroad.

The collision near Baker Bridge involved two trains. The first was a local passenger train composed of a single engine and tender, a combination car and three coaches. It had departed Boston at 7:16 p.m. on the railroad's

Fitchburg Division and was headed for the company's branch line to Marlborough. Eventually crashing into its rear end was the Montreal Express, which had two engines, two milk cars, two baggage cars, a mail car, a Pullman sleeper, a smoking car and two coaches. It left Boston, also via the Fitchburg Division, at 7:45 p.m.[65]

By the time Lincoln station was approached, and owing to the faster speed of the express, about five minutes separated the two trains. However, this was reduced to one minute owing to the slower-moving local train, which had delays. To alert any following train, the flagman, on the rear car platform of the local, threw out a series of red fusees: just before the station at Lincoln, another after the train made its station stop there, followed by yet another just before the station at Baker Bridge—this in accordance with company train rules.

At Lincoln, the railroad had installed two "spacing" signals: one at the Great Road crossing (a half mile east of the station) and another at a street crossing beside the station. The signals helped keep trains apart. Both displayed a green light to engineer Horace Lyons of the express. In fact, the engineer stated in his testimony that he definitely saw the green spacing signals and the red fusees and, importantly, knew the meaning of such. However, the engineer on the second engine of the express insisted in his testimony that Lyons never slowed down or applied the train's brakes upon realizing the express was getting closer and closer to the local.

About one hundred yards ahead of the local, Lyons first saw the red rear-end markers of its last car. He immediately threw the train brake into emergency, but a rear-end collision proved unavoidable. Prior to the accident at Baker Bridge, Lyons had a clean record; however, most of his experience was that of a locomotive fireman. He was currently just a spare engineer who did not hold a regular job and was called to work only when needed. Nevertheless, the thirty-seven-year-old was familiar with the division and its characteristics and had passed exams on such. But his actual experience as an engineer was extremely limited—just several months.

The impact of the collision was heard a mile away from Baker Bridge station. The first locomotive of the express telescoped into the rear coach, killing and injuring many, while the second engine pushed all of the debris ahead into the next two cars, where more fatalities were recorded. The first locomotive was completely destroyed. The crash also took the life of the fireman in the first engine. Live coals from the firebox of the first engine quickly spread fire to the Marlborough train, which was soon ablaze. Messages were immediately sent out for doctors, nurses, medical supplies,

fire apparatus and railway workers. Nearby residents of Baker Bridge also aided the rescue efforts. The majority of the injured were women.[66]

An inquest was conducted with testimony taken from thirty-one witnesses. Reporters were not allowed in the courtroom. Lyons was charged with manslaughter. The railroad commissioners of Massachusetts also conducted a public investigation, but it was obvious from the beginning who caused it. The case against Lyons was even brought before a grand jury, which acknowledged his guilt but chose not to indict him.[67] After termination, the engineer later worked for the Boston Elevated Railway. He died in Boston at age eighty-one and was interred in Saco, Maine.

Swampscott, February 28, 1956

Nearly seventy years ago, the Boston and Maine Railroad experienced an extremely sad disaster that brought upon the company—with good reason—a huge amount of negative publicity: the wreck at Swampscott. Incredibly, on the same day and on the same railroad, another rear-end collision occurred at Revere, but that story is not included here because there were no fatalities. Extraordinary as it may seem, several passengers managed to survive both wrecks! The Swampscott accident resulted in the death of 11 passengers and 2 train employees; 260 passengers and 10 train employees were injured.

Train No. 214 was a first-class passenger train en route from Portsmouth, New Hampshire, to Boston. It consisted of a diesel road-switcher engine and five coaches along with one baggage/smoking car. All the cars were constructed of steel. The train departed Portsmouth at 6:40 a.m. and passed the Salem, Massachusetts interlocking tower (junction of the Danvers Branch) at 8:10 a.m. Its speed was then reduced at signal P146 because the signal's aspect was obscured by snow and the engineer was unable to determine its indication until the train was almost upon it. The next two signals (P138 and RA2) were likewise covered with snow, to the extent the engineer could not see a light in either signal. Nevertheless, the train passed P138 at a low speed and stopped at signal RA2. Two or three minutes later, the rear of No. 214 was struck by train No. 2406 about 2,100 feet east of the station at Swampscott. No. 214 was due to leave that station at 7:54 a.m., about twenty-four minutes before the accident occurred.[68]

No. 2406, also a first-class passenger train, was en route from Danvers to Boston. It consisted of three diesel-powered passenger units and one diesel-powered passenger/baggage unit. All were so-called rail diesel cars (RDCs) built by the Budd company of Philadelphia. The train was held at the Salem tower until No. 214 went by. After it did so, No. 2406 went past the tower and entered, at 8:12 a.m., the railroad's Eastern Route division. It then passed signal P146, which displayed a "Prepare to Stop at Next Signal" indication, and then passed signal P138, which displayed a "Stop Then Proceed at Restricted Speed" signal. Inexplicably, the train did not stop at the latter and charged ahead at forty to fifty-five miles per hour, whereupon it plowed into the rear of train No. 214. No. 2406 was to have left Swampscott station at 8:08 a.m.—about ten minutes before the collision took place.

Train 214 was pushed ahead fifty feet by the impact. When the impact occurred, the underframe of its rear car overrode the lead Buddliner unit of No. 2406. Other damage was incurred by both trains, with several cars becoming mangled and thrown about. The engineer and fireman of No. 2406 were killed, and a number of trainmen were injured. In fact, all the fatalities that day occurred in the lead Buddliner unit. No employee on train No. 214 died, but many were injured.

A heavy, wet snow was falling at the time of the wreck, which took place at 8:18 a.m. The diesel-powered Buddliner units of No. 2406 were constructed

A dramatic image of the rear-end collision at Swampscott. Clearly seen is the single-car, self-propelled Buddliner that plowed into a standing train. Crowds gather to watch the removal of the deceased and injured.

of stainless steel, with the engines mounted under the floor of each unit. An operator's control station was located at each end of each unit. Each had disc-type brakes. The train's flagman had been dropping lighted red fusees at various points beyond Lynn tower to warn following trains of its presence. When the train was stopped by the red signal (RA2), the flagman exited the train with a red flag to stop any oncoming train.

Train 2406 was held at Salem tower for about fourteen minutes while waiting for No. 214 to pass. After it did so, it entered—as noted—the Eastern Route and stopped at Salem station. Its equipment was examined at the wreck site by an accident investigator of the Interstate Commerce Commission about two hours after the accident. In the wrecked operator's control compartment, the handle of the automatic brake valve was found to be in the emergency position.

The investigation report issued by the commission concluded that all signals were operating properly; that the colored roundels of signals were covered with snow; that B&M operating rules clearly stated that trains could only proceed past a snow-covered signal roundel at restricted speed—not to exceed fifteen miles per hour; that the Swampscott accident was caused by failure to operate the following train in accordance with signal indications; that the following train was operated at an excessive rate of speed; and that there was no appreciable deceleration of the following train before the accident occurred.[69]

The memory of the Swampscott disaster still lingers, especially with those who lost family or loved ones, not to mention certain railroad devotees. Trains still come and go in Swampscott and hopefully will continue to do so for many long decades to come.

Everett, December 28, 1966

Our concluding event in the Bay State, which also took place on the Boston and Maine Railroad, is like no other in this work. It involved a single self-propelled rail diesel car—a Buddliner, as discussed in the Swampscott wreck—which crashed into a stalled tanker truck (tractor and trailer) at a street crossing in Everett. Thirteen persons perished in the collision (eleven train passengers and two trainmen), which was jointly investigated by the National Transportation Safety Board in Washington, D.C., and the Public Utilities Commission of Massachusetts.

The fuel truck, owned by Oxbow Transport Company, was carrying at the time of the crash some 8,300 gallons of No. 2 fuel oil, which, when ruptured, ignited and sprayed much of the contents on the forward section of the Buddliner. The deaths therein were due to thermal burns and smoke inhalation rather than collision injuries. "The truck driver had left the vehicle prior to the collision and was not injured."[70]

Train No. 563 proceeded over a drawbridge about two miles west of the Second Street crossing in Everett at 12:08 a.m. and then accelerated to nearly sixty miles per hour. About nine hundred feet west of the street crossing, upon seeing the stalled tanker truck, the engineer threw the train brakes into emergency. At about fifty miles per hour, the Buddliner struck the tanker truck. The crossing was guarded by flashing red lights, a bell and a gate. They were not activated when the tractor and tanker entered the crossing but became so after it stopped across the tracks. The weather was clear, the temperature was about twenty-two degrees above zero and there was about four inches of snow on the ground.

The National Transportation Safety Board determined that the probable cause of the wreck was a loss of air pressure in the brake system of both the tractor and its trailer. The board also determined that most of the deaths and injuries on the Buddliner were due to the lack of emergency exits in the car, in addition to the inward-opening center rear door becoming jammed in the closed position because of persons attempting to escape.

The accident took place on the Boston and Maine route between North Station in Boston and Rockport, a distance of thirty-five miles. The route has two main line tracks: the inbound track (to Boston) and an outbound track. The collision occurred on the outbound track, about four miles east of North Station in Boston within the city limits of Everett. A crossing watchman was normally on duty at Second Street during the day, but not at the time of the wreck. The crossing itself, paved with bituminous material, was in a deteriorated condition, its surface uneven and pitted. Passenger vehicles passing over it often experienced a bumpy ride.

As we learned from the previous story, Buddliner units were made of steel and had operating controls in the vestibules at each end of the car. A "dead-man's pedal" was part of such. When the engineer raised his foot and released the pedal, an emergency application of the brakes would occur. An entrance/exit door for passengers existed at each car end.

Oxbow Transportation, owner/operator of the tanker truck, was based in Lexington. The tanker truck in the collision was not subject to the Motor Carrier Safety Regulations of the Interstate Commerce Commission. The

The Boston Globe

MORNING EDITION

WEDNESDAY, DECEMBER 28, 1966

Buddliner, Oil Tanker Collide, Burn

12 Die in Everett Train-Truck Crash

By LAWRENCE CURRAN
and JONATHAN BLAMFELD
Staff Reporters

BLACKENED TRUCK AND TRAIN AT SECOND ST. CROSSING. (Dan Sheehan Photo)

"The gates came down . . . the train was coming. We ran up the tracks to flag it down . . . It whizzed right past and then, wham! It was awful."

EYEWITNESS CARMEN ADDONIZIO
OF EVERETT—PAGE 23

List of Dead, Injured

DEAD

JOSEPH R. MUNSELL, 42, of 41 Belfast st., Buffalo, N.Y., pronounced dead at Whidden Hospital.

EDWIN P. MUST, 43, of 8 Hartford st., Belvidere, conductor of Buddliner, pronounced dead in Whidden Hospital.

INJURED

JOSEPH CAMPBELL, 31 Ash st., Danvers, critical condition, at Massachusetts General Hospital.

JOHN McEUEN, 21, of 7 Ellsworth st., Cambridge, fair condition, at Massachusetts General Hospital.

CHARLES R. VAN ALSTINE, 42, of 160 Nahant st., Lynn, fair condition, at Massachusetts General.

BRUCE JOHNSON, 38, of 19 Riverdale pk., Gloucester, burns on hands, face, fair condition at Chelsea Memorial Hospital.

RENEE E. LAUTENBERGER, 19, of Quincy st., Magnolia, severe burns, on danger list at Massachusetts General Hospital.

TRAIN CRASH
Page 23

Architects Ruling Called Predictable

By EDWARD J. ROWAN

ARCHITECTS
Page 4

Mrs. JFK 'Most Admired' Again

By GEORGE GALLUP

What Is It?

NOT THE BODY

Call 282-1800

LBJ's Version Of Dallas

By AUSTIN SPIVAK

LBJ
Page 3

No Sales Tax Rider

Volpe Gets Mental Health Bill Today

By CHRISTOPHER LYDON
Globe State House Bureau

MENTAL
Page 4

The Top Ten

Springfield's $6 Million Held

Bombing Criticism Frets U.S.

By BOB HORTON
Associated Press

BOMBING   Page 37

WESTMORELAND

BOSTON

THE PRESIDENT

DEC RUSK

Tension, Doubts Besiege Capital

By CHALMERS M. ROBERTS

APPRAISAL, Page 38

truck, slightly over forty-eight feet, was 3,555 pounds overweight, according to weight limitations prescribed by regulations in Massachusetts. The brake system had a warning buzzer, which sounded if air pressure was below 60 pounds. If below 30, the brakes would be fully applied automatically.

Upon seeing the stalled tanker truck, the engineer applied the emergency brake and then dashed into the forward part of the Buddliner to warn passengers of an impending collision. A few seconds later, the collision took place. The Buddliner partially derailed and stopped 158 feet east of the collision point. The tank of the semitrailer ruptured on impact and ignited, and a portion of its cargo was thrown on the forward section of the Buddliner. An intense fire and smoke ensued, which spread to the right side of the rail car. The interior of its forward section caught fire.

The explosion got the attention of two nearby Everett policemen, who were on the scene in minutes. They and the trucker attempted to break a window of the Buddliner but could only smash the outside pane and not the second one, which was made of laminated safety glass. By now, the rail car had filled with thick, black smoke, and everyone inside was in dire need of air. By breaking side windows in the car's smoking section with axes and bars, rescue operations finally began.

Realizing that his truck had stalled in a precarious position, the driver stopped a motorist and asked him to call the police. The warning apparatus at the crossing then began to engage. Along with the truck driver, both ran down the track to warn the approaching train, the motorist waving a white coat. The Buddliner, however, did not stop. They returned to the derailed train just as the policemen arrived.

Because of the extensive damage the tractor incurred, it was not possible for government investigators to conclusively determine what caused the tractor and tanker to stall on the crossing. But as previously noted, they concluded the "probable" cause was the loss of air pressure in the brake systems of both the tractor and the trailer, which resulted in an automatic application of the brakes that could not be released. Needless to say, an enormous amount of sympathy went out to the families of the deceased.

CHAPTER 5

VERMONT

Northfield, December 11, 1867

Two railroad disasters that claimed more than a dozen lives have taken place in the Green Mountain State: one at Northfield and the other in West Hartford. Both involved bridges. The first occurred on the Vermont Central Railroad, the latter on its 1872 successor, the Central Vermont Railroad.

The catastrophe at Northfield bordered on the bizarre. We begin its story with a somewhat remarkable comment by the then railroad commissioner of Vermont, William Rounds, which appeared in his 1868 annual report to the state's General Assembly:

> *I have not given as much time or attention to the examination of bridges as I should have done had I been an experienced bridge builder, until within the past year. Vermont roads have never contributed to the catalog of railroad disasters that from time to time have shocked the entire country. The catastrophe which occurred at Northfield on the 11th day of December 1867 was of that character. Legislation cannot now prevent it. The likes of it without legislation will never occur again. It has become part of the history of our Railroads, there it must remain as an ever-present admonition to railroad managers and operatives of the unyielding necessity—in the management of railroads—to always exercise every possible precaution against the reoccurrence of similar calamities.*[71]

On December 7, 1867, a live ember escaped from a passing locomotive of the Vermont Central and proceeded to burn down the so-called Harlow Bridge, which spanned a chasm some three hundred feet in width. The imposing structure sat on three stone piers—one at each end of the bridge and one in the middle. A road passed under the bridge (today's state Route 12A), as did the narrow Dog River. The end abutments were sixty feet tall, the center pier about seventy-five feet tall. The bridge was located about a mile and a half south of Northfield proper.

As the fire severed the main line of the Vermont Central, it became paramount to rebuild the bridge as fast as possible. Until completed, a temporary footbridge was installed between the end abutments, which forced passengers to disembark from one train and walk across the footbridge, only to reboard an awaiting train on the other side—this in the dead of winter!

A workforce of nearly one hundred men soon appeared on the scene to rebuild the burned structure. Supervising the work were Major Harvey Tenley, a master bridge builder, and Horace Locklin, the railroad's assistant superintendent. The problem of housing and feeding the workers was solved by shuttling them back and forth between the work site and Northfield proper, whereupon they walked to the Northfield Hotel. Their transportation from the construction site consisted of a locomotive and tender and a solitary passenger car. Occasionally, train runs were made with flat cars, on which building materials and supplies were conveyed.

Frank Abbott, a fifteen-year railroad veteran, was the engineer of the shuttle train on December 11. Having brought about sixty workers to the hotel for lunch, he was now returning them to the work site. As usual, the train moved in reverse to reach the bridge. For whatever reason, however, Abbott lost sense of how fast he was moving and did not, at first, heed the warnings to slow down from his fireman. The doomed train kept increasing speed until Abbott finally realized what was happening and slammed on the train brake and reversed the driving wheels. But it was too late.

The engine halted in time, but the passenger car with workers continued over the open abutment and crashed down into the Dog River, followed by the tender, which fell on the carnage. Eighteen workers were killed and forty were injured. Surviving workers and those already at the work site, along with nearby neighbors, rushed to aid the injured and extricate the deceased. Heavy ropes were used to raise up the dead and injured to land above.

Witnesses claimed that Major Tenney and engineer Abbott had words that day over the latter tardily sounding the locomotive whistle to get workers back on the train and for not moving the trains fast enough. As far as it is

RAILROAD DISASTER NEAR NORTHFIELD, VERMONT.—[PHOTOGRAPHED BY R. M. M'INTOSH.]

The rebuilding of the Harlow Bridge in Northfield after the previous one burned down. A lone passenger coach of a worker's shuttle train and its locomotive tender toppled from the granite embankment pier at left.

known, no investigation report of the accident was released by the railroad, nor was one published by Vermont's railroad commissioner. The county coroner, however, likely conducted an inquest. Why Abbott behaved as he did that fateful day remains inexplicable. His employment on the railroad was terminated. Work resumed rebuilding the bridge, and once completed, train service over the "new" Harlow Bridge commenced.[72]

WEST HARTFORD, FEBRUARY 5, 1887

The Central Vermont Railroad incurred its share of train wrecks and accidents during the nineteenth century. But nothing surpassed the dreadful 1887 disaster at West Hartford. Here, on a frigid winter night, a popular passenger train had one of its sleeping cars derail before the lofty Woodstock Bridge over the White River. The car dragged along the track, where, on the bridge, it fell over and crashed onto the frozen river below, dragging with it other cars. The carnage quickly caught fire due to overturned coal stoves and broken mineral oil lamps. Incredibly, the flames of the conflagration reached upward and ignited, and then fully destroyed, the bridge, which fell piecemeal to the frozen river below. The horrific tragedy took the lives of thirty-nine persons and injured fifty others. It was the second-deadliest railroad disaster to occur in New England's history, the first being at South Norwalk, Connecticut, in 1853.

Passenger train No. 50, the Montreal Express, left the White River Junction, Vermont station of the Central Vermont at 2:10 a.m., bound for Montreal, Province of Quebec. It consisted of a locomotive and tender; a baggage car; a combination mail and smoking car; a coach car from Boston; another coach from Springfield, Massachusetts; a sleeping car from Springfield named St. Albans; and a sleeper from Boston named Pilgrim. The train, which was running one hour and thirty minutes late that early morning, was scheduled to meet its southbound counterpart (Montreal to Boston) at a sidetrack in Randolph, Vermont.[73]

That early morning, the Montreal Express had seventy-seven passengers aboard. Some twenty-six persons were in the Boston coach; twenty-seven were in the Springfield coach; eight persons were in the Springfield sleeper; and thirteen were in the Boston sleeper. Among the trainmen were a conductor, an engineer, a fireman, two brakemen, a baggage man, an express messenger, two postal clerks, a Pullman conductor and two Pullman porters.

The distance from White River Junction to the West Hartford bridge (or Woodstock bridge, as it was sometimes called) was about four miles. South of the structure, which crossed the White River, existed a curve that became straight about 140 feet before the bridge itself and continued straight after the bridge was crossed. Per company rules, the engineer of the express had reduced the train's speed to less than fifteen miles per hour as he approached the bridge, which had to be sustained until the entire train had passed over the structure.

Suddenly, without warning, the rear sleeping car (Pilgrim) was thrown from the rails due to a broken rail about five hundred feet from the bridge's southern abutment. Despite being derailed, it bumped along the ties (or roadbed) until it came upon the bridge, whereupon its right rear end then swung off the bridge's deck and crashed down about forty-three feet to the frozen river below. To make matters worse, it dragged along the sleeper St. Albans and the two coaches ahead of St. Albans. Everything was crushed on the ice.[74]

As noted, fire broke out in various places in the wrecked cars, and within fifteen minutes, the entire wreckage was enveloped in flames. The flames eventually reached upward to the bridge's underside, which also became an inferno. The entire structure became engulfed in fire and crashed piecemeal down to the frozen river and wreckage below. "The intensely cold weather—eighteen degrees below zero—added to the peril of those who survived. Twenty-four passengers would die in the disaster along with six trainmen including the train's conductor, Smith Sturtevant of St. Albans, Vermont."[75] There was but one house some distance from the disaster. The only rescue help at hand were the few who were left on the engine, the baggage and mail car and coach passengers who were not disabled.

Conductor Sturtevant, in his last moments, was in the forward passenger coach collecting fares and examining tickets when the first trouble in that car was noticed. He immediately pulled the bell cord, whereupon engineer Pierce instantly applied full brakes. Then, looking back, Pierce saw the rear sleeper swing off the bridge. He then let off the brakes, opened the throttle and pulled away from the rest of his train, stopping his engine and the two cars once on land. Once stopped, the engineer dispatched Brakeman Parker

The scene at West Hartford after the Montreal Express crashed through the bridge to the frozen White River below. Fire erupted, which proceeded to burn the downed train and the bridge.

to get help. Pierce and others then took axes and shovels and hurried down the snow-covered embankment to rescue the suffering, until they were driven from the wreck by the flames. News of the disaster was sent to the railroad's office in St. Albans and to the state's railroad commissioners, and several arrived at the wreck site while it was still smoldering. The commissioners began a formal investigation that Monday in White River Junction. Forty-one witnesses would furnish testimony.[76]

The bridge over the White River was of a double Towne lattice design, 26 feet deep, 650 feet long. It consisted of four spans of 140 feet and a short span of 70 feet. The piers and abutments were made of Vermont granite. The distance from the track to the surface of the ice was 42 feet; the bottom of the trusses were 16 feet from the water's surface.[77]

The railroad commissioners found no fault with the train crew or its actions. Rescue efforts by them were commendable. There were no defects in the bridge per se, nor was it poorly constructed. The commissioners were convinced, however, that the cause of the disaster was a broken rail south of the southern abutment, which struck the central journal of the forward truck of the sleeper Pilgrim. The commissioners also concluded that the actual fracture in the broken rail could not be observed or detected until disclosed by the breaking of the iron. Lastly, they felt that had not coal stoves and oil lamps been in use, which ignited the varnish, paint, draperies and so on in the cars and sleepers, many of the fatalities would not have occurred. The solution lay in steam heat from the locomotive and electric lights.

Naturally, lawsuits arose against the Central Vermont Railroad because of the West Hartford disaster. But not all litigants would receive compensation because of legal footwork and court delays. Those who did often got paltry settlements.[78]

Today, trains of the New England Central Railroad (a subsidiary of Genesee and Wyoming) rumble across the White River bridge, where an incredible tragedy unfolded so long ago.

CHAPTER 6

NEW HAMPSHIRE

West Canaan, September 15, 1907

Railroad history began in beautiful New Hampshire—a state known for its inviting seashore, majestic lakes and sky-piercing mountains—in the 1830s. The first line to open was the Nashua and Lowell Railroad in 1838, which at Lowell connected with the Boston and Lowell Railroad for a valuable entrance into Boston. Railway construction continued in the Granite State, and one of the more noteworthy lines completed was the Northern Railroad, which connected the capital city of Concord with White River Junction, Vermont ("Junction"), by way of the New Hampshire settings of Andover, Danbury, Canaan, Enfield and West Lebanon. At the Junction, physical connections were made with the Central Vermont and the Connecticut and Passumpsic Rivers Railroad for Montreal and other points in Quebec. In 1899, the Northern became part of the legendary Boston and Maine Railroad (B&M).

By 1907, the year of the West Canaan disaster, the B&M was operating some 2,200 miles of mainline track, 528 miles of secondary mainline track and 1,282 miles of sidings. In New Hampshire, it owned 181 miles of railroad and leased 857 miles. More than 5,000 B&M employees resided in the Granite State, and approximately 1,500 B&M stockholders called the state home. As the railroad commissioners of New Hampshire stated in their 1907 annual report, the Boston and Maine Railroad was "distinctively and almost exclusively New Hampshire's railroad."

Gross revenues of B&M would amount to $41.1 million in 1907; expenses came to $31.9 million, and net earnings totaled $10.1 million. All its passenger cars were equipped with air brakes; 99 percent of its freight car fleet also had them, and all its steam locomotives were so equipped. Some 160 miles of the system now had automatic block signals for the protection and safety of train movements. However, none were yet installed on its Concord Division, from Concord to the Junction. Had they been, the catastrophe in West Canaan would have been prevented.

Like almost every American railroad, the B&M had its share of wrecks, accidents and disasters. Its safety record in New Hampshire was relatively good, as its railroad commissioners noted in their 1907 annual report:

> *From July 1, 1883, to September 15, 1907, only two persons were killed or fatally injured in the passenger cars of the steam railroads in New Hampshire. This remarkable record, which we think was unparalleled in the transportation of as many railroad patrons as traveled upon our roads in twenty-four years, was ended by a head-on collision near West Canaan, Sunday morning, September 15, in which twenty-six persons lost their lives and seventeen others were seriously hurt.*[79]

The single-track Concord Division—sixty-nine miles in length—had twenty-four miles of sidings where opposing trains could safely meet one another. By 1907, traffic on the division was down some 50 percent since 1892, primarily because freight manifests were frequently routed over the company's White Mountain and Fitchburg divisions. Nevertheless, some twenty-eight regular passenger and freight trains utilized the division each week plus several extra trains, the fewest number in all B&M divisions.

Train movements over the division were controlled by the dispatcher in Concord, whose office was located on the second floor of the company's imposing brick station designed by Bradford Gilbert, architect of Grand Central Station in New York City. A telegraph operator occupied an office on the first floor. Trains were operated by telegraphic train orders (over the signature of the division superintendent) and timetable authority. The operating rules for the company were those established by the American Railway Association, which were used by 85 percent of all American railroads. The dispatcher's office was continuously manned (24/7), as were several telegraph/station offices on the division, including Franklin, East Andover, Canaan, Enfield, West Lebanon and the Junction. On weekends, when traffic was slow, the third track Concord dispatcher doubled as the telegraph operator, it being his additional responsibility to go downstairs to meet train crews, deliver train orders, relay messages and so on.[80]

On Sunday morning, September 15, 1907, James Browley was on duty as the Concord Division dispatcher and telegraph operator from 11:00 p.m. the night before to 7:00 a.m. Browley had been dispatching trains for six years and was a telegraph operator for eighteen years. Up at Canaan station, John Greely—another key player in the disaster—had twenty-three years of experience as a telegraph operator. Greely was working a twelve-hour shift that day, which had begun at 7:00 p.m. Saturday night to 7:00 a.m. on Sunday morning, with one hour off for dinner. Both men had proven reputations for being safe, competent, sober and loyal.

On Browley's desk was a chart or train sheet that showed the location of all trains currently in the Concord Division. It was incumbent upon dispatchers to enter on it—among other items—the arrival and departure times of trains at the various stations when such information was reported by the telegraph operators. Also on his desk was the train order book, the official record of all train orders the dispatchers issued for the safe movement of trains over the division. Among the myriad kinds of orders were those fixing the location of meeting points between opposing trains.

Back in that era, a train order was not first written down by the dispatcher but initially conceived in his head and telegraphed to the appropriate operators. When the initial operator repeated back the train order, only then would the dispatcher write down the order in the train order book. Each word and number would be underscored by the dispatcher each time an operator would repeat the order. If more than one operator received the order, each had to wait their turn to repeat it. If an operator correctly repeated it, the dispatcher would reply "O.K." along with the time. Some train orders, such as so-called "31" train orders, required the operator to obtain the signatures of the conductor and engineer before their train could proceed. After the operator confirmed he had obtained such signatures, the dispatcher would then transmit the word "Complete" along with the time, whereupon the train could depart. Train orders and messages that did not require signatures (called "19" orders) were often "hooped up" by the operator to the engineer and conductor of a passing train, or they were handed to crew members inside the telegraph office.[81]

In the early morning of the West Canaan disaster, three trains had Browley's attention: northbound freight No. 267 (Concord north to the Junction) and two southbound passenger trains from the Junction to Concord and Boston, Nos. 30 and 34. Where the freight train would meet the two passenger trains was growing in importance, as both were running late and their usual meeting points with No. 267 would have to be changed. All three were regularly scheduled trains appearing in the company's employee timetable.

No. 30—the Quebec and Boston Air Line Express or Quebec Express—had been delivered to the B&M at the Junction by the Connecticut and Passumpsic Rivers Railroad. That morning, it was full of passengers, many of whom were returning home from the Quebec Fair in Sherbrooke, Quebec, which that year was combined with the Dominion Exhibition. Many of the passengers on board resided in the French-Canadian communities of New Hampshire and Massachusetts. No. 34, the Montreal Express, had originated in Montreal and been delivered to the B&M at the Junction by the Central Vermont Railroad. Normally, No. 30 would depart ahead of No. 34, the latter following about thirty minutes later.

Freight train 267 had left Boston the evening before and departed Concord (on September 15) at 12:45 a.m. for its northbound trip to the Junction. Upon leaving Concord, the train consisted of a locomotive and tender along with twenty-seven cars, most of which were loaded with merchandise or commodities. Benjamin Lawrence was the train's conductor; engineer Elisha Shurtleff was in the locomotive cab.

It was the duty of James Maher, the telegraph operator at the Junction, to keep Browley informed about the two passenger trains. Because each was running late that morning, Browley sent a telegraphic train order at 2:18 a.m. to each at the Junction (care of Maher) and the operator at East Andover, where freight train No. 267 was soon due. The order stated that No. 30 would run forty minutes late from the Junction to East Andover and that No. 34 would run thirty minutes late from West Lebanon to Concord. Such information would allow the freight train to safely advance beyond East Andover to a location farther up the line to meet the two trains.

After leaving the Junction at 3:55 a.m., No. 30 made station stops in New Hampshire at West Lebanon, Lebanon and Enfield—the last station before Canaan that had a nighttime telegraph operator. Upon receiving its copy of the train order, freight train 267 departed East Andover and arrived at 4:10 a.m. in Canaan, where Conductor Lawrence felt it best to safely meet No. 30. However, while No. 267 was advancing toward Canaan, Browley received fresh information from Maher regarding passenger train No. 34: it would now be forty minutes later than first thought, for a total of one hour and ten minutes.

To alert everyone of the changes, Browley then telegraphed train order No. 4 (at 3:38 a.m.) to No. 34 while it was still at the Junction, to the operators at East Andover and Canaan and to train 267. It stated that No. 34 would run one hour and ten minutes late from West Lebanon to East Andover and one hour late from East Andover to Concord. This meant that No. 267 could now safely advance beyond Canaan to West Canaan, where it would meet No. 34. But a problem arose: Browley could not immediately ask Greely, the operator at Canaan, to copy the order, for he had stepped away from his telegraph instruments. Nevertheless, he transmitted the order to Maher and No. 34 at the Junction and the operator at East Andover.

About eight minutes later, Browley reached Greely and told him to place his train order signal to red (which he did), meaning that freight 267 had to stop at Canaan for train orders. Once Greely confirmed his train order signal was set at red, Browley reached for the train order book and resent the order he had just sent to the Junction and East Andover. It read:

> Order No. 4, September 15, Canaan, N.H.
> To: C. & E. 267
> No. thirty (30) will run one (1) hour and ten (10) minutes late West Lebanon to East Andover.

But in doing so, Browley made a fatal error: he mistakenly telegraphed to Greely that No. 30 would be running one hour and ten minutes late when he should have telegraphed about No. 34. Greely, who was not privy to the position of all the trains on the division, repeated the order to Browley exactly as he had received it, whereupon Browley O.K.'d it at 3:46 a.m. (No other nighttime operator on the division heard the mistake.) When No. 267 stopped at Canaan, conductor Lawrence and engineer Shurtleff proceeded to the telegraph office and signed the train order. Greely reported this to Browley, who made the order "Complete" at 4:15 a.m. Both crew members then reboarded their train and departed Canaan at 4:20 a.m. to meet No. 30 at West Canaan, four and a half miles to the north, with plenty of time to spare. They were totally unaware that No. 30, which had briefly stopped at nearby Enfield at 4:21 a.m., was now barreling down to West Canaan.

In railway parlance, Browley had created the dreaded "lap of authority," a situation in which a dispatcher makes a mistake and loses control of a train, with a disaster often resulting. One of the tragic features of many railway accidents is that once a blunder has been made, opportunities for saving the situation get lost. In this situation, Browley failed to seize two such opportunities. First—having O.K.'d Order No. 4 to Greely at 3:46 a.m.—he had over a half hour to correct his error before No. 267 departed Canaan at 4:20 a.m. Second, even after No. 267 departed Canaan, Browley had until 4:21 a.m. to telegraph the operator at Enfield to hold or flag down No. 30 from going down to West Canaan.

The countryside around West Canaan was especially dark in the pre-dawn hours of September 15. It was also very foggy. A thick mist had settled on the landscape during the night and coated the rails of the Boston and Maine Railroad. No. 30, the Quebec Express, was now advancing south at thirty to thirty-five miles per hour after briefly stopping at Enfield (above West Canaan) at 4:21 a.m. Freight train 267, which left Canaan at 4:20 a.m., was now pounding north at about twenty-five miles per hour to the siding at West Canaan, where it would meet No. 30.

That morning, the Quebec Express consisted of a locomotive and tender, a baggage car, a coach, a smoking car and a Pullman sleeping car. About 150 passengers were aboard the train. Having passed West Canaan, engineer Callahan soon rounded a curve and approached a covered bridge. Just as his train entered the wooden structure, he saw—to his horror—the headlight of No. 267 coming directly at him. He immediately applied the emergency train brake and, with his fireman, jumped out of the cab to the ground below while the train was still moving. (The engineer and fireman of No. 267 did likewise.) According to the accident report by the state's railroad commissioners, "Eighteen hundred feet from the west end and fifty-four hundred feet from the east end of the straight track, the two locomotives

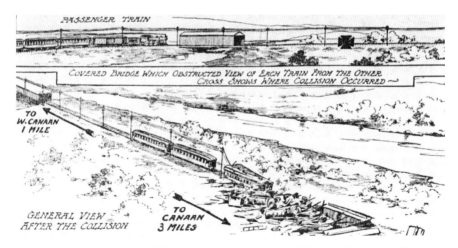

A diagram of the head-on collision between two Boston and Maine trains at rural West Canaan, the deadliest of all New Hampshire train wrecks.

collided, completely wrecking themselves, smashing a number of the freight cars, and driving the baggage car through the passenger coach killing twenty-six passengers and injuring twenty others."[82]

The commissioners also noted in their accident report that

> *had the weather been fair and clear that morning, it is altogether possible that both engineers, seeing the headlight of the oncoming trains the moment the passenger swung upon the straight line or when they were 3,600 feet apart, by prompt action could have slowed down so that the collision would have been prevented or the results would have been much less serious. As it was, the fog made it impossible to see more than 300 to 400 feet, and when the engineers threw their brakes into emergency and shut off the steam, the wheels slid instead of rolling over the slippery rails without greatly reducing the speed or lessening the force of the impact.[83]*

The head-on collision shook the ground, and the grinding of steel and iron, mixed with the splintering of wood and timbers, shattered the early morning air. As one newspaper reported:

> *The two locomotives reared when they met, crushing each other in a thunderous burst of steam. They both fell over to the south of the track, still locked together. At the same time, the heavy Pullman sleeper was thrusting the day coach forward resistlessly. The baggage car, made of a stiffer material than the day coach right behind it, plowed bodily through the coach and ground the crowded, sleeping passengers to death. There was a terrible shrieking of tortured humanity mingled with the roaring of escaping steam. Then, the wreck settled together, and for a moment there was dreadful quiet. Men crawled from the wreckage. The locomotive crews appeared, limping from where they had fallen as they leaped from their cabs just before the crash. A flare lamp began to flicker about the indiscriminate heap that had been two locomotives.[84]*

A goodly number of the freight cars forming No. 267 crashed into one another during the collision and were promptly tossed down the track embankments, their contents scattered.

Those still alive and mobile within the day coach began attending to the seriously injured and trapped passengers. Once extracted from the wreckage, they were placed along the track embankment to receive first aid. (Makeshift bandages were fashioned from Pullman bedding sheets.) Passengers who

WHERE LIVES WERE LOST.

BAGGAGE CAR AND DAY COACH.
Heavy Baggage Car Was Forced Into and Through the Lighter
Day Coach, Leaving, However, a Space Above the Floor of the Day
Coach Into Which Many Passengers Were Thrown, So That They
Escaped Alive.

Most of the casualties at West Canaan occurred when the heavy baggage car of the Quebec Express telescoped into the day coach. Men, women and children perished.

had perished were placed either alongside one another on the opposite embankment or in the Pullman. "The loading of the train of death had been a gruesome spectacle. Their limbs were dangling at strange angles from the planks that served as biers, the straggling heap falling into the seats of the car. The little children were handed in through a car window."[85]

Among those experiencing the calamity firsthand was Frank Sibley, a Pullman passenger who was a reporter for the *Boston Globe*. That paper, for days on end, covered the wreck story with photographs, drawings, interviews and railroad press releases. Sibley heard passengers begging for whiskey to ease their pain, while other survivors dealt with broken seats and splintered timbers amidst the crying and moaning of women and children. He saw a baby taken away while prattling to its dead mother. Seat cushions had been pushed through broken windows. Some of the severely injured and incapacitated offered money, diamonds and watches for assistance in getting off the train.

Conductor Brown of the Quebec Express, who was thrown about in the wreck, managed to recover and walk back to West Canaan station, where he had calls placed to area physicians, who soon appeared with their "medical cases and little needles of morphia." (The doctors advanced to the wreck site in horse-drawn carriages.) The off-duty station agent at West Canaan was found and notified dispatcher Browley in Concord about what had happened.

Passenger train No. 34, which was following No. 30, was flagged down at West Canaan to prevent a rear-end collision. Two locomotives were hauling the train, and Brown convinced the lead engineer to uncouple his engine, proceed to the wreck site and pull back the Pullman sleeper to West Canaan. Upon the car's arrival, several of the injured were taken to area farmhouses and hospitals. Later, No. 34 made its way back to White River Junction, where it was rerouted down to Claremont Junction to Concord. Word of the disaster quickly spread, especially in the French-Canadian communities of Massachusetts. At 5:00 p.m., No. 34 pulled into Lowell, where literally thousands were on hand looking for injured or deceased friends, neighbors and family members. A similar scenario would unfold at North Station in Boston.

Once informed of the wreck, Browley telephoned William Ray in Concord, superintendent of the Concord Division, whom he awoke from a sound sleep. (He had to explain to Ray no fewer than three times what had happened in West Canaan.) Ray then notified B&M officials in Boston and at once organized an ambulance corps, summoned medical professionals and assembled a wreck train with workers and equipment. The trainload of surgeons, doctors, nurses and railroad employees arrived at the wreck site at 7:22 a.m. Ray admirably took charge of the carnage and had the main track cleared by 3:30 p.m. that day for passing trains. Those passengers on No. 30 who were seriously injured or had perished but had not been brought to West Canaan were brought back to Concord in the coach attached to Ray's train. At the ready in the capital city were personnel at the Pillsbury Hospital and the city morgue.

Once at the wreck site, Ray tried to unravel what events or factors might have caused the calamity, as far as engines, cars, tracks and personnel were concerned. Nothing seemed unusual or out of order, and he concluded that a mistake in train orders was the probable cause. Boston and Maine Railroad officials from Boston appeared, and for several days, investigative interviews were conducted in secret with train employees and with dispatcher Browley in Concord and Greely, the telegraph operator in Canaan. Both men were temporarily taken out of service.

According to one newspaper, Browley and Greely declared in the investigations that they were innocent of any mistake or wrongdoing. After combing through records, train orders and evidence at Concord, Canaan and elsewhere, railroad officials became "baffled" at which man caused the

Officials of the Boston and Maine became baffled over who caused the West Canaan disaster: either a train dispatcher or a telegraph operator. The state's railroad commissioners would cite the dispatcher.

disaster. However, they did agree that no employee on trains 30 or 267 had erred or shied away from their responsibilities and duties.[86]

This conundrum hardly baffled the railroad commissioners of New Hampshire, who began a public investigation of the wreck from September 24 to October 3, held at Phenix Hall in Concord to accommodate a large crowd. During that time, employees and officials of the B&M were called to testify, including Browley and Greely. Once again, the records, drawings, train orders and other evidence were minutely examined. The three commissioners (Henry Putney of Manchester, Arthur Whittemore of Dover and George Bales of Wilton) issued their report, which the *Boston Globe* ran word for word on October 12. Unlike B&M officials who could not or would not name which man was at fault, the commissioners concluded that no error had been committed at Canaan by operator Greely or by the crew of freight train 267. However, they did cite dispatcher Browley as having made a mistake in issuing order No. 4 to Greely and No. 267. Whereas the train order book showed the correct train number designations, Browley had mistakenly telegraphed to Greely No. 30 instead of No. 34.

What prompted Browley to make the fatal error will never be known, nor is it known why he would never admit to having made a mistake. Perhaps he became confused, or playing both dispatcher and operator at Concord that morning weighed too much on him. It also is still inexplicable why B&M officials could not identify Browley (at the end of their investigations) as having caused the disaster, especially considering their vast accumulated experience in uncovering the root causes of train wrecks.

In an interview with Browley at his Concord home on September 18, the *Boston Globe* reported that there was much sympathy in the city for the dispatcher over what had happened, he being "a prominent secret organization man and a popular fellow in general." He insisted in the interview that he had made no mistake.

Two asides: the death toll at West Canaan climbed to twenty-six persons after Albina Jauron of Nashua, New Hampshire, died of injuries at the Hitchcock Hospital in Hanover. On a happier note, the wreck brought together—at the same hospital—Anthony Jacques and Delina King, both widowed, of Millbury, Massachusetts. After being discharged, the couple married.

CHAPTER 7

MAINE

Onawa, December 20, 1919

For many Americans, the state of Maine—biggest of the New England states—is a world unto itself. It boasts a beautiful rocky coastline, stunning mountains, sparkling lakes and rivers, endless forestlands of spruce and pine and unlimited recreation such as hiking, skiing, fishing, hunting, swimming and boating. It is the only American state having a single syllable. One can live here happily removed from society, or one can be extremely sociable. The accent of its natives is unmistakable, their humor witty and dry. Timber and shipbuilding first drove Maine's economy; pulp, paper, potatoes and textiles followed. Railroads were slow in arriving as oceangoing vessels and assorted rivercraft would reign supreme for decades.

In 2023, a handful of major, regional and small railroad companies serve Maine, plus tourist lines and Amtrak. The Canadian Pacific Railway once serviced the state but exited in the 1990s, only to return to the fold in 2020.[87] And it was that firm that experienced a little over a century ago the deadliest railway disaster that the Pine Tree State has ever faced. It occurred just west of remote Onawa, in sprawling Piscataquis County—a head-on collision between a freight and passenger train that killed twenty-three persons and seriously injured fifty others.

Onawa is found on the Canadian Pacific Railway's Moosehead Subdivision (of its Brownville Division), a single-track route that ran between

Brownville Junction northwesterly to Lac-Megantic, Province of Quebec, a distance of nearly 120 miles. Train movements over the line were governed by train orders and timetable authority, except for two small sections where a permissive staff block system was used. Train orders were transmitted to station operators by telephone from the train dispatcher's office at Brownville Junction, found about 18 miles east of Onawa.

The disaster took place on a sharp curve two and a half miles west of Onawa station. A mountainside borders the inside of the track curve; Little Greenwood Pond sits about fifteen feet below the outside of the curve. The engineer of an eastbound train could see the curve about seven hundred feet beforehand, while a westbound engineer could not see it until almost on it. The wreck, which took place in clear weather just after daybreak, involved two trains: westbound passenger train Third No. 39 and eastbound freight train First No. 78.

Third No. 39 was en route from St. Johns, New Brunswick, to Montreal. It consisted of (in this order) an engine and tender, one box-like baggage car, one coach, two "colonist" cars, two tourist cars, another colonist car, one café car, another tourist car and two cabooses. Some three hundred immigrants (mostly English and Scottish) were on the train, along with Canadian soldiers. The immigrants had disembarked the day before from the steamship *Empress of France* at St. Johns. Likely, many were headed for the prairie lands of Saskatchewan or perhaps Alberta. One newspaper reported that the immigrants were "well-dressed and had a large quantity of baggage."[88]

Conductor Dillon was in charge of this immigrant special; Engineer Wilson was in the locomotive cab. Both men left Brownville Junction with several train orders containing important information about other trains also running on the division. It was the duty of the train dispatcher to keep train crews informed about one another, especially where opposing ones would safely meet one another. It left Brownville at 6:25 a.m., some five hours late, and passed Onawa station at 7:00 a.m., five hours and ten minutes late. Around 7:14 a.m., while moving at twenty-five to thirty miles an hour, it collided head-on with eastbound freight train First No. 78, not far from Onawa station.

Conductor Manuel was in charge of First No. 78; Engineman Bagley was in the cab. The train was formed with a locomotive and tender, plus thirty loaded freight cars, two empty freight cars and a caboose. It had left Lac-Megantic the night before at 6:00 p.m. and set out cars at various points on its southeasterly journey. It safely met several westbound trains, including one at Moosehead whose crew handed off a copy of a train order to Manuel that, among other information, let him know that Third No. 39 (the immigrant special) was running five hours late. When Manuel and Bagley arrived at Greenville at 6:30 a.m., ten miles east of Moosehead, they received yet another copy of the same order. The freight train left Greenville at 6:40 a.m., and Manuel and Bagley decided to meet the immigrant special at Morkill, six miles east of Greenville. Then, something strange unfolded.[89]

After the head brakeman got off the engine and opened the siding switch at Morkill, Engineer Bagley eased the freight train into the passing track (at 6:57 a.m.), only to meet, on foot, station operator Kingdon holding a fresh train order (No. 47), the gist of which noted that westbound passenger train "Fourth" No. 39 was running eight hours late. In testimony, Kingdon insisted he yelled, "Fourth No. 39 eight hours late," while handing over the train order to the engine and caboose crews. But for whatever reason, the crew members either misheard Kingdon or misread the train order and concluded that it was Third No. 39 running eight hours late. Wrong! The freight train kept moving through the siding, reentered the main line and went ahead farther east to Brownville Junction, where their sixteen-hour shift would soon end. However, about two miles west of Onawa station, while running at twenty to twenty-five miles an hour, it collided head-on with Third No. 39, the immigrant special.

The carnage at the four-degree curve was nothing less than horrific. Both locomotives interlocked, the baggage car was demolished and the engine, tender and seven cars of the freight train derailed. The coach car telescoped into the first colonist car for about two-thirds its length. The wreckage then caught fire, and two of the coaches and the baggage car went up in flames. Engineers Bagley and Wilson and their firemen (Henniger and Hutchins) perished in the disaster. Seventeen immigrants were killed outright, and six died after being removed from the wreck. Six of the twenty-three fatalities were children. A special train was soon rushed to the scene, and most of the fifty individuals injured were taken back to Brownville Junction and received treatment in the railroad YMCA. Twenty were later sent to hospitals in Bangor.[90]

According to the investigation report of the Interstate Commerce Commission, Conductor Manuel and (the late) Engineer Bagley of the freight train caused the disaster. Also censured were crew members of Manuel's train who misread the train order and operator Kingdon, who knew fully well the freight train should never have left the siding at Morkill. Train dispatcher Shaw, in turn, was reprimanded for not paying closer attention to

Little photographic evidence exists of the head-on train wreck at Onawa. This deteriorated image depicts the locomotives having just been pulled apart and re-railed.

the trains underway in his division. (Some forty daily trains passed over the Moosehead Subdivision.) The government investigator recommended that a better, safer block signal system be adopted.

Today, a small crop of stones and a wooden cross mark where the Onawa disaster occurred. Every day, trains of the Canadian Pacific Railway rumble past the memorial. Likely few, if any, of the train crews know what happened here that frigid December morning in 1919. For certain, though, they know that not far away is a more memorable landmark: the breathtaking steel and concrete bridge over Ship Pond Stream—the highest and longest trestle in the state of Maine, perhaps in New England.

NOTES

Chapter 1

1. Sidney Withington, "The Strange Case of Robert Schuyler," *Railway and Locomotive Historical Society, Bulletin No. 98* (April 1958): 32–46.
2. *The Report of the Board of Directors of the New-York and New-Haven Rail Road, 22 August 1849* (New York: H. Cogswell, 1849), 27.
3. "The Norwalk Catastrophe, Verdict of the Jury," *New York Times*, May 11, 1853, 2.
4. Frank Briggs Jr., "Norwalk Bridge Disaster," *Structure Magazine*, February 2020.
5. Wreck details are extracted from articles appearing in the *New York Times* beginning May 7, 1853.
6. Michael Mittlemann, MD, "Dr. Gurdon Wadsworth Russell's Account of the 1853 Railroad Accident at Norwalk, Connecticut," *Connecticut Medicine* 64, no. 5 (May 2000): 291–97.
7. Find a Grave, "Edward Tucker," www.findagrave.com/memorial/173115344/edward-tucker.
8. *Twenty-Sixth Annual Report of the Railroad Commissioners of the State of Connecticut for 1879* (Hartford, CT: Case, Lockwood and Brainard, 1879), 3.
9. Holbrook, *Story of American Railroads*, 282.
10. Ibid.
11. Gregg M. Turner and Melancthon W. Jacobus, *Connecticut Railroads: An Illustrated History* (Hartford: Connecticut Historical Society, 1986), 130–54.

12. *Twenty-Sixth Annual Report…of Connecticut*, 4.
13. Turner, *Connecticut Railroads*, 139.
14. "Tariffville Disaster," *Hartford Daily Courant*, January 16, 1878, 2.
15. "The Late Railroad Disaster," *New York Times*, February 24, 1878, 3.
16. George L. Vose, *Bridge Disasters in America* (Boston: Lee and Shepard, 1887), 36–37.
17. Mark Aldrich, "Another Wreck on the New Haven," *Social Science History* 39, no. 4 (Winter 2015): 613–46.
18. Interstate Commerce Commission, *Report of the Accident Investigation Occurring on the New York, New Haven and Hartford Railroad, Bridgeport, Connecticut. July 11, 1911*, 2–3. Wreck details herein are extracted from this report.
19. "12 Die in Wreck, 47 Injured, on Boston Flier," *New York Times*, July 12, 1911, 1–2.
20. Ibid.
21. "Widow of Engineer Curtis Claims He Had Been Over Worked by Railroad Company," *Bridgeport Evening Farmer*, July 11, 1911, 1.
22. Interstate Commerce Commission, *Report of the Accident Investigation Occurring on the New York, New Haven and Hartford Railroad, North Haven, Connecticut, 2 September 1913*, 1–2. Wreck details herein are extracted from this report.
23. "Sleeping Home Comers Victims of Rear-End Collision," *New York Times*, September 3, 1913, 2–4.
24. *Interstate Commerce Commission, Report of the Accident Investigation…2 September 1913*.
25. "Wilson Sees Wreck Pyre," *New York Times*, September 3, 1913, 2.

Chapter 2

26. "Awful Railroad Accident," *New York Times*, August 13, 1853, 8.
27. "The Railroad Slaughter," *New York Times*, August 13, 1853, 2.
28. "Railroad Disaster, Verdict in the Railroad Case," *New York Times*, August 10, 1853, 3.
29. "Doings at the Rhode Island General Assembly at Newport," *New York Times*, September 27, 1853, 2.

Chapter 3

30. Charles Welton Felt, *The Eastern Railroad of Massachusetts: Its Blunders, Mismanagement and Corruption* (Liverpool, UK: Miss J. Green, 1873), 3–24; *Third Annual Report of the Massachusetts Board of Railroad Commissioners, January 1872* (Boston: Wright & Potter, 1872), xcv–cv. Wreck details herein are extracted from this report.

31. *Third Annual Report…1872*, xcv–cv.

32. Holbrook, *Story of American Railroads*, 278–82.

33. Ibid.

34. Adams, *Notes on Railroad Accidents*, 125–43.

35. *Third Annual Report…1872*, xcv–cv.

36. Ibid.

37. Holbrook, *Story of American Railroads*, 278–82.

38. *Ninth Annual Report of the Board of Railroad Commissioners, January 1878* (Boston: Rand, Avery & Company, 1878), 37–43. Wreck details herein are extracted from this report.

39. Ibid.

40. "Terrific Railroad Crash," *New York Times*, October 9, 1878, 2.

41. Adams, *Notes on Railroad Accidents*, 7–8.

42. Ibid.

43. *Nineteenth Annual Report of the Board of Railroad Commissioners, January 1888* (Boston: Wright & Potter Printing, State Printers, 1888), 90–112. Wreck details herein are extracted from this report.

44. Ibid.

45. Frank Griggs Jr., "Bussey Bridge Disaster, aka Forest Hills Bridge, 1887," *Structure Magazine*, June 2021, 58–59.

46. *Special Report by the Massachusetts Board of Railroad Commissioners to the Legislature, in Relation to the Disaster on March 14, 1887, on the Dedham Branch of the Boston & Providence Railroad* (Boston: Wright & Potter Printing, 1887), 247.

47. Available on Amazon.com and books.Google.com.

48. *Special Report by the Massachusetts Board…*, 4–420.

49. Ibid., 22–25.

50. "A Novel Railway Accident," *Harper's Weekly* 32, no. 1622, January 21, 1888, 47–48.

51. *In Relation to the Accident on the Western Division of the Boston & Maine Railroad, at the Junction of the Georgetown Branch with the Main Line Between Bradford Station and the Bridge over the Merrimac River, on Tuesday, the 10th*

of January 1888. Annual Report of the Railroad Commissioners of Massachusetts for 1888, 176–98. Wreck details herein are extracted from this report.

52. Ibid.
53. Ibid.

Chapter 4

54. *Twenty-Second Annual Report of the Board of Railroad Commissioners, January 1891* (Boston: Wright & Potter Printing, 1891), 113–32. Wreck details herein are extracted from this report.
55. Ibid.
56. Ibid.
57. "Wreck on the Old Colony," *New York Times*, August 20, 1890, 2.
58. Ibid.
59. *Twenty-Fifth Annual Report of the Board of Railroad Commissioners, January 1894* (Boston: Wright & Potter, 1894), 136–55. Wreck details herein are extracted from this report.
60. Ibid.
61. Ibid.
62. Ibid.
63. Ibid.
64. "Train and Bridge Went Down," *New York Times*, September 1, 1893, 1.
65. *Thirty-Seventh Annual Report of the Board of Railroad Commissioners, January 1906* (Boston: Wright & Potter, 1906), 57–65. Wreck details herein are extracted from this report.
66. "16 Killed, 25 Hurt in Blazing Wreck," *New York Times*, November 27, 1905, 2; "Rear-End Collision Brings Death to 17," *Boston Daily Globe*, November 27, 1905, 1.
67. "Engineer Is Not Indicted," *Boston Daily Globe*, December 9, 1905, 2.
68. *Interstate Commerce Commission, Ex Parte No. 200: Accidents at Swampscott and Revere, Mass, Decided May 16, 1956*, 1–20. Wreck details herein are extracted from this report.
69. An outstanding video about the wreck, expertly narrated by railroad historian Richard Symmes, can be viewed on YouTube, titled "Remembering the Swampscott Wreck of 1956."
70. *Boston and Maine Corporation Single Diesel-Powered Passenger Car 563 Collision with Oxbow Transport Company Tank Truck at Second Street Railroad–Highway*

Grade Crossing Everett, Massachusetts December 28, 1966 (Washington, D.C.: National Transportation Safety Board, 1968), 1–56. Wreck details herein are extracted from this report.

Chapter 5

71. *Report of the Railroad Commissioner of the State of Vermont for 1868* (Montpelier, VT: Poland's Steam Printing, 1868), 3, 4.
72. Paul Heller, "Horror All Over the Land—Northfield's Harlow Bridge Tragedy," *Times Argus*, December 7, 2016, 2. Certain details herein are extracted from this excellent article.
73. *First Biennial Report of the Board of Railroad Commissioners of the State of Vermont, December 1, 1886, to June 30, 1888* (Boston: Rand Avery Company, 1888), "Hartford Bridge Accident," 91–100. Wreck details herein are extracted from this report.
74. Ibid.
75. Ibid.
76. Ibid.
77. Frank Griggs Jr., "West Hartford (Woodstock) Bridge Disaster," *Structure Magazine*, May 2021, 34–35.
78. J.A. Ferguson, "The Wrong Rail in the Wrong Place at the Wrong Time: The 1887 West Hartford Bridge Disaster," *Vermont History* (Vermont Historical Society) 81, no. 1 (Winter–Spring 2013): 52–74. This article is noted for its outstanding scholarship and readability.

Chapter 6

79. *Sixty-Third Annual Report of the Railroad Commissioners of the State of New Hampshire, 1907*, xiii.
80. Ibid., xxv.
81. Details about Concord Division operations and the West Canaan disaster are extracted from the above railroad commission report, 345–55.
82. *Sixty-Third Annual Report… State of New Hampshire, 1907*, 348.
83. Ibid.
84. "Railroad Wreck at West Canaan, New Hampshire," *Boston Globe*, September 16, 1907, 4.
85. Ibid.

86. "Problem Staggers Railroad Officials," *Boston Globe*, September 18, 1907, 1.

Chapter 7

87. Justin and Timothy Franz, "CP Comes Full Circle in Maine," *Railfan and Railroad Magazine*, August 2020, 46–57.

88. "C.P.R. Train Wreck Kills 23, Injures 50—Freight and Immigrant Special in Head-on Collision in Maine," *New York Times*, December 21, 1919, 1.

89. *Interstate Commerce Commission, Report of the Accident Investigation Occurring on the Canadian Pacific Railway, Onawa, Maine*, December 20, 1919. Wreck details herein are extracted from this report.

90. Ibid.

SELECTED BIBLIOGRAPHY

Adams, Charles Francis, Jr. *Notes on Railroad Accidents*. New York: G.P. Putnam's Sons, 1879.

Aldrich, Mark. *Death Rode the Rails: American Railroad Accidents and Safety, 1828–1965*. Baltimore, MD: Johns Hopkins University Press, 2009.

Baker, George Pierce. *The Formation of the New England Railroad Systems*. Cambridge, MA: Harvard University Press, 1937.

Chandler, Alfred D., Jr. *The Visible Hand: The Managerial Revolution in American Business*. Cambridge, MA: Belknap Press of Harvard University Press, 1977.

Grant, Ellsworth S. *Connecticut Disasters*. Guilford, CT: Morris Book Publishing, 2006.

Holbrook, Stewart H. *The Story of American Railroads*. New York: Crown Publishers, 1947.

Kirkland, Edward Chase. *Men, Cities and Transportation: A Study in New England History*. Vols. I and II. Cambridge, MA: Harvard University Press, 1948.

Nock, O.S. *Historic Railway Disasters*. London: Arrow Books, 1986.

Reed. Robert C. *Train Wrecks: A Pictorial History of Accidents on the Main Line*. Atglen, PA: Schiffer, 1997.

Rolt, L.T.C. *Red for Danger*. London: David & Charles, Ltd., 1976.

Shaw, Robert B. *A History of Railroad Accidents, Safety Precautions, and Operating Practices*. Kirkwood, NY: Vail-Ballou Press, 1978.

ABOUT THE AUTHOR

Gregg Turner, a Connecticut native and collegiate educator, has had a lifelong interest in trains, railroading and railway history. He has authored over a dozen award-winning books and numerous articles, largely on the enterprise of transportation. A graduate of Mitchell College, Eastern Connecticut State University and Rensselaer Polytechnic Institute, he is a former curator and board member of the Railway and Locomotive Historical Society at Harvard Business School. Now a resident of Fort Myers, Florida, he can be contacted at greggturner@msn.com.